Praise for *Why We Travel*

'If you like travel you must read this! A beautiful, insightful
and thought-provoking book with the power to change
how you see travel – and life. Ash is a thought-leader in the
travel space and it's not hard to see why. Simply brilliant'
Pip Stewart

'*Why We Travel* is an eloquent journey, exploring the
very essence of life and the motivations we have for
travelling. Navigating and blending real world adventures
with the landscapes of our mind. You'll find profound
meaning and insights with every step of the journey,
that isn't just about the destination. An excellent read'
Aldo Kane

'Ash is a great storyteller, whose book weaves together
adventure, big ideas and inspirational tales from around
the world. A must for any smart-thinking traveller'
Levison Wood

'*Why We Travel* is the right book at the right time,
interrogating the biological and social reasons
we wheel our suitcases out ... Bhardwaj is out
to change mindsets, not just itineraries'
The Bookseller

'What a story!... We don't often hear about the long and rocky road that separates a journalist's dream from readers and listeners. *Why We Travel* will inspire and help others who would like to share their passion for discovery. It's personal, adventurous and shines with curiosity'
Nicholas Crane

'A beautiful book. *Why We Travel* will catch you unawares in the most unexpected ways. While it will certainly make you a more thoughtful and better traveller, there's a high chance it will make you a more thoughtful and better person, too'
Alex Bescoby

Why We Travel

A Journey into Human Motivation

ASH BHARDWAJ

Bedford
Square
Publishers

First published in the UK in 2024 by
Bedford Square Publishers Ltd,
London, UK

bedfordsquarepublishers.co.uk
@bedsqpublishers

A CIP catalogue record for this book is available from the British Library.

ISBN
978-1-915798-78-7 (Hardback)
978-1-915798-79-4 (Trade Paperback)
978-1-915798-80-0 (eBook)

2 4 6 8 10 9 7 5 3 1

Typeset by Palimpsest Book Production Ltd, Falkirk, Stirlingshire

Printed in Great Britain by CPI Group (UK) Ltd, Croydon CR0 4YY

For Mother B

Introduction

For all its material advantages, the sedentary life has left us edgy, unfulfilled. Even after 400 generations in villages and cities, we haven't forgotten. The open road still softly calls, like a nearly forgotten song of childhood.[1]
Carl Sagan, *Pale Blue Dot*

Travel is the driving force of my life. It's my career, my hobby, my love and my nemesis. When I was a child, we rarely went on holidays abroad, but I explored the countryside near our home with the enthusiasm of a Labrador, and I loved it when Mum took us to visit her brothers in Devon and Holland. At the age of 17, I had my first proper overseas adventure. It was life-changing, and I have been preoccupied with travel ever since.

I have travelled in many different guises: as a backpacker and as a soldier, on expedition and on holiday, in groups and on my own, for work and for fun. I went for sport and for love, as a journalist and as a pilgrim, a teacher and a student, and I learned as much about myself as I did about the world. Travel was my gateway to ideas and education.

As I built a career in travel journalism, I began thinking about the *purpose* of elective and leisure travel (as against migration for economic or security reasons). For many people, travel sits alongside homeownership and marriage as a significant life goal, and we Brits spend more on package holidays than we do on any other leisure activity.[2]

Given that we spend so much of our time either travelling or saving up to go travelling, it seems surprising that we rarely think about *why* we do it. Most travel marketing focuses on fun and relaxation, but when I reflect on my own travels I realise that this only captures a small proportion of my adventures.

This means that we miss out on much of what travel can do for us. We live in an era when travel is not just getting more expensive, but also causing catastrophic climate change, ruinous amounts of waste and irreversible habitat destruction. It is time for us to think more carefully about when we travel and why.

As I reflected on my own reasons for travelling, I became curious about why other people travelled. I started by asking my friends and colleagues, then I interviewed scientists, philosophers, DJs and athletes. I read everything from historical poetry to religious texts, and I became acquainted with niche scientific research. It was an incredible journey into the minds of others, and I brought some of their motivations into journeys of my own.

Why We Travel is the result of that mission. Each chapter is a mix of travelogue, conversation, advice, research and self-reflection. Most of the travels are my own. Some are epic adventures, others are closer to home, and some are journeys of internal exploration. Each is a window into a specific motivation for travel: Curiosity, Inspiration, Happiness, Mentorship, Serendipity, Hardship, Service, Empathy, Healing, Wonder, Eroticism and Hope.

I unpack these motivations through interviews, research and the science of their origins. I use them to explore other journeys, and topics ranging from genetics to psychedelics. I look at how travel intersects with the rest of our lives, and question its hold over us: Why do we travel? How do we do it 'better'? Can it help us to live more fulfilling lives?

I have come to realise that no one motivation is 'better' than any other. Instead, we travel with different motivations at different times, and they sometimes overlap. Some of them will be familiar to you, and others might seem absurd or outlandish. But I hope that they inspire you to think about travel differently.

I also hope that they give you an insight into where our motivations come from, and how they affect us in everyday life. Because these motivations are not just reasons to travel – they are reasons to live.

Ash Bhardwaj, November 2023, London.

Chapter 1

CURIOSITY: From Windsor to Waikato

Windsor was a good place to grow up, even if you weren't royalty.

Throughout my childhood, hundreds of thousands of tourists came to the town every year, thanks to our famous local resident, Her Majesty Queen Elizabeth II. At 11 a.m. each day, the soldiers of the Household Division – dressed in their scarlet tunics and bearskin hats – would march behind a band from their barracks to Windsor Castle, for the Changing of the Guard ceremony. After drinking in this display of military pomp, the tourists would file into the castle, and enjoy the Queen's interior design.

Familiarity may not breed contempt, but it tends to breed disinterest, as I didn't even visit the castle until my early twenties. But our famous neighbour had her positives: the castle's Crown Estate provided easy access to nature. The tourist industry meant lots of jobs in hospitality. And teenage delinquency was limited to eating Woolworths pick'n'mix without paying.

I had gone to the local junior and middle schools, then won

a scholarship to do my GCSEs at a Quaker boarding school in Reading. I did well academically, but I only had a few friends, and I always felt dislocated, so I chose to return to the local state system for my A levels, and joined the Windsor Boys' School in 1999.

Not long after I started at Windsor Boys', my mum discovered that the school was planning a rugby tour to Australia, New Zealand and the Cook Islands. She told me that, if I got a place on the team, she would pay for my place on the tour.

Mum had travelled to New Zealand in the 1970s, and she loved it. She inspired me with stories of smoking volcanoes, empty beaches, trees unchanged since the time of the dinosaurs, and wildlife that had evolved in isolation from the rest of the world. It sounded magical, and my excitement was matched by my teenage desire for independence: I would be travelling with my peers and without my family, but within the safety net of an organised tour.

Mum had raised my sister Barty and me by herself. We lived on income support in social housing and, while we never struggled for food or clothing, we didn't go on fancy holidays or buy expensive junk for the house. But Mum felt that it was important for me to have experiences that broadened my horizons, so she took on a second job as a cleaner, just to cover the cost of my ticket.

All I had to do was to learn how to play rugby.

In my late teenage years, I was a slightly overweight geek, more focused on hip-hop and science fiction than on drop-goals and scrums. Most of my friends were metalheads and skaters who sat around in parks, getting stoned and drinking cider.

With a goal to achieve, things began to change. I spent evenings at rugby training instead of the local park, and watched rugby games on the telly, rather than *Star Trek*. I also had to get fit for the first time in my life, so I trained at the school gym every morning.

I could barely catch a ball at my first rugby session, but I kept turning up and doing what the coaches told me to. I played as a prop because it mostly involved just leaning on other people, and because no one else wanted to do it. I was given a place as a substitute and slowly got better and fitter, until I eventually made it into the starting line-up for the second team. I would be going on tour.

The day of departure was nerve-wracking. I was about to spend three weeks further from home than I had ever been before, with a group of near-strangers who had been mates with each other for a decade. A large part of me didn't want to go because I was nervous that I wouldn't have a 'place' within the group.

The two teams played six games each during the tour, and we stayed in the family homes of our opponents, rather than hotels. That meant we had to come out of our shells and speak to locals, instead of hiding at the back of a group. It also meant that we experienced things that most tourists would never see, so we got to know each country at a deeper level than most visitors.

Nowhere was this more apparent than in New Zealand, which I had basically thought of as a far-flung outpost of Britain in the southern hemisphere: they spoke English, ate lamb, had the Union Jack on their flag, and they even played rugby and cricket. Australia's indigenous Aboriginal people had been almost invisible during our visit there, and I assumed that the same would be true of New Zealand's indigenous Māori.

My preconceptions were shattered from the moment we arrived: Auckland airport signs appeared in Māori as well as English, and our coach driver, Bernie, told us legends about Polynesian gods stalking the land and ocean. When we arrived at Ōtūmoetai College, the students greeted us with a Māori haka that put goosebumps on my arms.

Once the formalities of that greeting were over, both groups milled around like boys and girls at a school disco, our local hosts on one side of the room, and us, the touring party, on the other. Curiosity got the better of me, and I was the first to cross the gap, to start asking the Kiwis about their cultural mix.

'It's just the way things are,' said my host, 'Māori and Pakeha (white New Zealanders) go to school together. We work together, we fall in love, we get married. There's still challenges, of course, but it means that Kiwi culture is a mix of both cultures.'

The next couple of days were enthralling. We explored the Bay of Plenty with our hosts, and hiked up Mount Maunganui, an ancient lava dome that was once the site of a fortified Māori village. At Rotorua, we saw bubbling mud pits and superheated geysers, before swimming in hot pools heated by the same geothermal activity.

The rugby games were a close-fought affair. As the second team, we always played the warm-up match, and we managed to win an ugly encounter of muddy tackles and dropped passes in pouring rain. Our first team were in the lead throughout, but they were foiled by the referee's scandalous decision to award a last-minute penalty to the hosts. The ball sailed through the posts and put an end to our winning streak.

As soon as the two games were over, any frictions from the

pitch disappeared, and we were all invited to one of the players' houses. They were preparing a hangi – an underground oven, in which volcanic rocks are heated on a bonfire in a pit. Once the flames had died down, food wrapped in leaves was placed in metal baskets above the rocks. Then everything was covered with wet cloths, buried in soil and left to cook in the heat.

A few hours later, the pit was dug up and the food unwrapped. The lamb was the tenderest that I'd ever eaten, and it came with seafood that one of our hosts had caught in the bay. We stayed until dawn, drinking beer, chatting to our opponents and getting to know our teammates. It was a ritual that we went through after every game that we played, in every town that we visited; making new friends and learning about their lives.

By the time we got back to Windsor, I was an integral member of a close-knit fraternity. We had forged bonds of allegiance through shared physical hardship and built memories that would stay with us for ever. For most of my teammates, the tour had been an extended holiday, with fun activities and novel things to buy. But, for me, it was life-changing.

There was something intoxicating about arriving in a place that felt subtly different to home, from the font on car number-plates to the way people greeted each other. By spending time in unfamiliar environments with a new social group, I uncovered skills and interests that I never knew I had.

'Ash was a great ambassador,' my coach said to my mum when we returned. 'He was always the first person to speak to the other team because he wanted to know everything about the places we visited.'

That single trip to the Pacific was a revelation. I found a

world beyond skate parks and *Star Trek*, and I realised that asking questions – both meaningful and minor – made travel infinitely more rewarding. It taught me the power of curiosity in travel, which lit a fire inside me that has been burning ever since.

Humans live in every environment on Earth, ranging from the desert to the Arctic, but we are not born with the bodies or instincts to survive in most of them.

Simple animals, like flies, are born with innate behavioural responses. Complex animals, like lions, learn essential behaviours from their parents. These animals have had to adapt gradually to their environments through thousands of generations of natural selection. But we humans are different: we adapt to our environments through a mix of skills, knowledge and collaborative strategies that no single individual could ever figure out in their lifetime.[3]

Just think about the skills and knowledge of a remote tribe in the Amazon: the construction of shelter and making of clothes; knowing what plants to eat, and how to prepare them; animal-tracking to find prey; crafting bows and arrows, blowpipes and darts; collecting frogs' poison to hunt; preparing and butchering prey; and building fires to cook dinner.

This complex social knowledge is 'culture' and we learn it from other members of our societies. As humans develop new knowledge, it is passed on and improved in a kind of evolution that takes us beyond mere biology. This 'cultural evolution' means that we adapt much faster than other animals to new and changing conditions, which has enabled humans to reach every corner of the Earth (and even into space) in just 70,000 years.

Why am I telling you this in a book about travel? Because cultural evolution requires learning. Learning depends on curiosity. And curiosity makes us want to travel.

'Curiosity is defined as "an intrinsic motivation to learn",' says Dr Emily Emmott, an evolutionary anthropologist whose research focuses on adolescence. 'It's more than just copying – it's experimenting, to figure out how things work for ourselves. You see this in kids who repeat what adults say, but in a weird or funny way. No other species experiments like this.

'During adolescence, something changes in how we process information. We actually become more curious because we need to learn cultural and social knowledge for adulthood. That's why teenagers are curious about things that are permitted for adults but not children, like smoking. They are working out how to "adult".'

Curiosity differs from risk-taking. We take risks because there might be a benefit at the end of a dangerous activity. But with curiosity, there is no inherent danger, and we often seek out information that has no obvious purpose or reward. We just want to know what's out there, which affects our general behaviour, not just our response to specific incidents.

'Studies show that our "range" grows every year,' Emily says, 'As children get older, they start playing further from their house. As teenagers, they start to visit friends who live further away, and they want to see new places or experience novel things. They seek autonomy, as part of the preparation for adulthood, and curiosity is the driver.'

This spatial component of curiosity was vital for early humans who needed to migrate for space and resources. For that to happen, someone in their tribe had to wonder what was over the horizon – and be willing to take a look. Human societies that contained such 'curious' individuals became more likely to survive, so the trait was more likely to be passed on. But why are some people more curious than others?

In 1999, a variation of the gene DRD4 was linked by researchers to adventure, curiosity and restlessness. By 2012, we knew that it was found in 20 per cent of modern humans, but it occurred more frequently in populations that had experienced a lot of migration. The variation (DRD4-7R) became known as the 'wanderlust gene' when the science writer David Dobbs suggested that it was linked to a specific passion for travel.

'Bearers of this mutation,' Dobbs said, 'are more likely to take risks; explore new places, ideas, foods, relationships, drugs, or sexual opportunities... they generally embrace movement, change and adventure.'[4]

So are those without DRD4-7R destined for life as a homebody?

Not exactly. In his BBC Radio 4 series, *Bad Blood*, the geneticist Adam Rutherford explained that, while some genes are essential to a trait, no single gene is deterministic, even for simple characteristics like eye colour. Behaviour is even more complex. It's a product of hundreds of our genes, as well as our upbringing, experiences, interactions and environment.

Think of it like the ingredients in a recipe: you can't make chicken tikka masala without chicken; but simply having chicken doesn't guarantee a tikka masala. You need all the right herbs and spices, cooked in the right way, in the right order, or you could end up with chicken soup. We all have the genes that allow us to be curious (DRD4-7R is just a 'boosted' version that makes curiosity more likely). We just have to 'cook' the genes that we have in the right way, through specific experiences and interactions.

'In some hunter-gatherer populations,' Emily says, 'children as young as three can choose to spend time with their aunts and uncles, and walk between family camps whenever they like. This freedom gives them the chance to stimulate their curiosity, and they become more curious as a result. But in less permissive societies, where children are more bounded by rules, they end up becoming less curious.'

The 'chef' for this recipe is the brain's limbic system, which is involved in emotional processing and rewards. It's what gives you that 'kick' from doing something you enjoy, thanks to a neurotransmitter called dopamine. Put simply, certain tasks or behaviours trigger the release of dopamine. That makes you feel good, which encourages you to repeat the task or behaviour.

This is why we like eating fatty and sugary foods. Our behavioural systems developed while we were still nomadic hunter-gatherers, who needed energy from fruits, nuts and animal fat. Our body evolved to release dopamine when we ate those foods, which made us feel good, encouraging us to repeat the behaviour of finding and eating those foods. We might not be hunter-gatherers anymore, but that behavioural feedback-system is still with us.

Curiosity is linked to the dopamine system in a similar way. When we discover something, and our curiosity is satisfied, we get a dopamine kick. Our unconscious brain learns that curiosity leads to feeling good, and it encourages us to repeat the activity that stimulates it.[5]

Dopamine systems must be triggered for a behaviour to be linked with that kick: people need to eat an ice cream to know that they like it, but, once they do, they go looking for it again. Perhaps the rugby tour to New Zealand rewarded my curiosity circuits in the same way. They learned that travel would give them a kick, and that's why I've been chasing it ever since.

Humankind's first form of travel was curiosity-driven migration, and most of it happened on foot: up through Africa, across the Sinai Peninsula, along the coast of Arabia, into Europe, down to India, and across the Ice-Age land-bridge between Russia and Alaska.

But the most remarkable migration happened by sea. And, because it occurred within the last few millennia, its story is recorded by its descendants, in oral history and legends.

Twenty years after the rugby tour, I returned to New Zealand's Bay of Plenty. It is home to Jack Thatcher, a Māori celestial navigator, who has spent his life researching traditional Polynesian sailing methods. He took me to Tauranga Marina, where his boat, the *Ngahiraka mai Tawhiti,* was undergoing repairs. The two hulls each had a carved red figure on their prow, and were connected by a deck that carried two masts.

'This is a waka hourua,' Jack said. 'A voyaging canoe, like the one Kupe used.'

Kupe was a legendary Polynesian explorer. While there are variations of his story in Māori oral traditions, they all agree that he came from the semi-mythical land of Hawaiki, and discovered the land that became New Zealand. Kupe and his wife named it Aotearoa, which means 'Land of the Long White Cloud.'

'New Zealand is remote,' Jack said. 'We're 1,200 miles east of Australia, and 600 miles south of Fiji and Tonga. It takes days of sailing to get here from anywhere else, but our ancestors discovered it around 1,000 years ago, and they did it without compasses, sextants, clocks or maps. Having found

Aotearoa, they then travelled back and forth – over and over again – to settle it. But that was just the end of a long voyage of curiosity and innovation.'

Around 3000 BCE, some humans in modern-day Taiwan began exploring rivers and deltas with dug-out canoes. To cross larger stretches of water, and to reach nearby islands, they began experimenting with outriggers to make their canoes more stable. At each island they reached, they could see another one on the horizon, and to cross these longer distances they developed skills of steering and sailing.

It took them 2,000 years to reach Samoa, Fiji and Tonga. But to go any further, they would have to cross wilder ocean.

'They guessed more islands were over the horizon,' Jack said, 'because they saw birds flying from that direction. But ocean-sailing was a big jump in skill and technology: they had to carry enough food to survive several weeks of exploration, on ships that could survive storms and sail against the prevailing wind.'

They built stronger, double-hulled, ocean-going canoes (like Jack's waka hourua), with shelters for safety and provisions. They developed new sailing techniques, navigated by the stars, and learned to find land through weather patterns, swells, sea animals, bird migrations, and even flotsam and jetsam in the water. New knowledge was learned, and their culture evolved, until they became the Polynesian wayfinders.[6]

Once they had cracked these skills and technology, the Polynesians quickly found the Cook Islands, Marquesas and French Polynesia. At the peak of their abilities, they used ocean

---

[6] This part of the story was memorably depicted in Disney's film *Moana* (2016).

currents to head north and south to Hawaii, Rapanui Easter Island, and eventually to Aotearoa, New Zealand. The historical existence of kūmara sweet potato in Polynesia (when it originates in the Americas) suggests that they may even have reached South America before Europeans did.

This is a perfect example of the cumulative cultural knowledge that Emily had told me about: each generation learned the skills, technology and strategies of their predecessors; then curiosity drove them to experiment, innovate, and cross thousands of miles of open ocean. Along the way, they evolved cultures that were perfectly adapted to their environments.[7]

'Today these techniques seem like magic,' said Jack, 'but they evolved over millennia, and took decades to master.

'Once our people settled in New Zealand, there were fewer voyages back to the islands, and our distinctive Māori culture developed. Our people still fished the oceans, and used inland rivers to get around, but the voyaging skills were lost, particularly after Europeans arrived.'

The legacy survives if you know where to look. In the Māori legend '*Kupe and the Giant Wheke*', Kupe is forced to chase a giant octopus (Te Wheke-a-Muturangi) from his homeland. As he pursues the wheke, it leads him to Aotearoa. He follows it down the east coast, through the Cook Strait and into Queen Charlotte Sound, where he kills it. Afterwards, Kupe heads up the west coast and returns home to Hawaiki.

'It sounds like a fairy tale,' said Jack, 'but it contains navigational knowledge. In the story, the wheke starts in Hawaiki – which is probably modern-day French Polynesia and the Cook Islands – and its tentacles are a metaphor for the ocean currents in that area, which our ancestors used to reach Hawaii, Rapanui and Aotearoa. The path of the battle with the wheke, and the stories around it, are a map of Aotearoa's sea conditions, safe harbours and places to settle.

'So it's a sort of guidebook, and the listener can learn everything they need to know about voyaging to Aotearoa from that legend. That's how our people pass down knowledge – through culture and stories.'

In 2012, Jack put these ideas to the test when he captained *Ngahiraka mai Tawhiti* and another waka, *Te Aurere*, on an 18,500-kilometre journey from Auckland to Rapanui Easter Island, over to French Polynesia and the Cook Islands, then back to New Zealand. He did the whole thing without modern instruments, and relied on the wayfinding and navigational techniques of his ancestors, and the knowledge of currents and places from Māori myths and legends.[8]

So it looks like curiosity is the architect of the travel bug. It evolved to help humans figure things out and adapt to new environments, and it pushed us to migrate. There is a genetic component to curiosity, but it needs stimulation to flourish.

What does this mean for us, as modern-day travellers? Can we use our understanding of curiosity to make travel more fulfilling?

The psychologist Professor George Loewenstein has shown that humans have 'a natural inclination to close information gaps'.[9] And the closer we get to solving a riddle, the more we want to do so. It's a craving, similar to the craving for drugs, sex, and sugary foods. And just like those other cravings, it requires a trigger. Something to spark that curiosity, and the desire to find an answer.

In *The Psychology of Curiosity*, Loewenstein suggests four ways to induce curiosity in humans:

1. The posing of a question, or presentation of a puzzle.
2. Exposure to a sequence of events with an anticipated, but unknown, resolution.
3. The violation of expectations that triggers a search for an explanation.
4. Knowledge of possession of information by someone else.[10]

When I discovered these four principles, I realised that they all exist in travel. When linked, they describe the template for a compelling travel experience:

1. The potential traveller poses the question: 'What is place x like?'
2. The journey rips them from the mundane routine of daily life. It is pregnant with possibility and unpredictable outcomes.
3. Everything that they encounter will be subtly different to the way it is back home, from ingredients in their dinner, to the colour of the sky. The traveller will want to know why.
4. The traveller seeks information from a source, such as a guidebook, a fellow traveller or a newspaper article. They want information that will help them see the 'real' face of their destination, and to acquire that knowledge for themselves.

Loewenstein's research also suggests that humans crave the answer to 'questions of no importance', which might be part of the appeal of travel. When we are away from home, we are surrounded by a million unimportant questions – *Why do they use that font on road signs? Why do they greet each other like that?* – so travel inherently appeals to our deep-rooted instinct of curiosity.

The ultimate expression of this quest for explanation is the desire to discover the 'real' version of a place. But there is no perfect answer because there is no such thing as the 'real India' or 'real London'; there are an infinite number of versions, based on timing and individual experience. So we keep looking for it, endlessly answering unimportant questions, and asking new ones out of curiosity, prompted by the craving and satiation of our dopamine system.

But how do we become curious in the first place? We can't do much about the DRD4-7R mutation – you either have it or you don't.[11] The good news is that, either way, it is not deterministic: you can be curious without having the DRD4-7R mutation; or you could have it, but be totally lacking in curiosity. It's your experiences that matter; curiosity needs some stimulation to get going, but then it becomes self-perpetuating.[12]

My own curiosity was stoked by childhood visits to my aunty and uncle's house in Maidenhead, where the scent of Indian cooking and the sound of spoken Punjabi transported me from suburban England to the subcontinent. It wasn't entirely my own culture – I was raised by my mum in an English household – but I loved it, and it made me curious about the link between culture and place.

---

[12] DRD4-7R probably makes some difference at the extremes of adventure and exploration, in the same way that genes related to muscles make a difference if we are sprinting at the Olympics. But most exploration is the equivalent of a casual half-marathon. In which case, training and practice matter much more than genetics.

This was deepened by Michael Palin's travel documentaries, which showed me places beyond my imagination. His charm brought out the best in the people that he met, and he revealed what disparate cultures had in common, not just how they differed.

These stories and experiences lit the embers of my curiosity, and the rugby tour added fuel to the fire. But if I had not taken that opportunity, given to me by my mum, my dopamine system might not have linked personal travel with curiosity, and the travel bug would never have bitten me. The first step on the path to curiosity lies in seizing opportunities.

*

Chay Blyth was a sergeant in the British Army's Parachute Regiment. One day in 1966, his boss, Captain John Ridgway, asked Chay to find him a volunteer to row the Atlantic as part of a world record attempt. Chay volunteered himself.

When Chay and Ridgway arrived in America, they were scheduled to do a promotional event in Boston Harbor, to build interest in their record attempt. But Ridgeway had fallen ill with food poisoning, so Blyth was on his own. The assembled journalists asked him to row a lap of the harbour, so that they could take some photos.

'Sorry,' said Chay, 'I don't know how to row.'

'You don't know how to row?!' said the journalists, 'But you're about to cross the Atlantic!'

'Exactly,' he replied, 'I'll have plenty of time to practise.'

They crossed the Atlantic in 92 days, encountering two hurricanes, several storms, cargo ships, sharks and whales. After surviving that feat, Chay sailed around the world single-handed, then founded the British Steel Challenge so that novice sailors could experience something similar. He became one of the greatest sailors in history, and was eventually knighted for his services to sailing. I was lucky enough to meet him at an event in London.

'When I committed to rowing the Atlantic,' Chay said, 'I didn't know it was going to change my life. I just knew that Captain Ridgway's offer opened the door to possibility.

'I knew very little about either the ocean or rowing when I signed up to do it. I had no idea what that life looked like, but I *did* know what life would look like if I *didn't* seize the opportunity – another few years in the garrison in the Far East, and maybe a promotion. I knew what *that* looked like because I'd already been doing it for eight years!'

'How does someone know what opportunity to say "yes" to?' I asked.

'These "opportunistic moments" present themselves everywhere,' Chay said, 'from spotting a job offer, to bumping into someone you fancy. There is a second or two to act, before the opportunity disappears for ever.

'You should apply for that job. Or say hello to your crush, even if you don't know the next step after that. You can usually figure out how to do it along the way – like I did with rowing. Even if you fail, you will never regret trying.

'But here's the thing: you never know which one might change your life. You might quit the job after two weeks, or it might become your calling in life. The date might go terribly, or they might be the person you marry.

'The only solution is to seize all those opportunistic moments while you still can, in case one of them is the winner. You can't win the lottery unless you buy a ticket!'

My opportunistic moment was my mum's bargain. I had no idea how I would get into the rugby team, but I said yes and then worked out how to do it. The journey was as important as the destination because I got fit, made new friends and discovered new skills along the way. But it became the opportunity that changed my life.

For travel, once you have seized that opportunistic moment and begun a potential adventure, you can apply Loewenstein's principles to invoke curiosity and ask, 'what's this place like?'.

To refine it, you could ask, 'what's different about here from home?'. Most of these are 'questions of no importance', such as the alert-sound of pedestrian crossings, or the number of adverts on television. But each piece of information will stimulate your dopamine system, rewarding your curiosity and building a habit.

Hobbies are a great shortcut because they open up communities and insights. As a teenager back in Windsor, I wanted to learn how to ride a horse. I couldn't afford lessons, so I volunteered to muck out the cavalry stables in Windsor Great Park. In return, they taught me how to ride. When I travelled to Australia, in 2006, I chose to take this further and got a job at a stud farm that bred racehorses.

The stud farm was in Queensland's Darling Downs, two hours east of the city of Brisbane. This was rural Australia, with spectacular sunsets and dramatic storms that steamed across the rolling countryside. I was taught to ride 'Western' style, learned Aboriginal tracking techniques, went to country fairs at the weekends, rode horses to country pubs, and saw sheep-shearers catch venomous snakes in woolsheds.

Just before I left Australia, I caught up with a friend who had been travelling up and down the east coast.

'I'm a bit envious,' he said. 'I've partied with loads of

different people, but the inside of one nightclub is pretty similar to any other. You've shown me that there's a whole different culture here – not just Britain with better weather and dangerous animals.'

From Australia, I moved to Wānaka, New Zealand, and joined a local rugby club. Wānaka is a ski town – full of seasonal staff – but my rugby teammates were locals. They were mostly farmers or builders who had grown up in the area, and they brought me into their lives by taking me hiking or hunting, and inviting me round for dinner. Every Saturday the team drove to isolated rugby clubs, in stunning locations that don't get mentioned in guidebooks. After the game we would hang out in the hosts' clubhouse, where my teammates would swap stories about bricklaying techniques and chasing escaped sheep. There could have been no better way to get to know the region and its people.

Once you've got used to asking 'questions of no importance', you might be curious about 'questions of *some* importance'. How did the climate and landscape affect the cultures that evolved here? Why are the animals like this? What is the main music of this region, and what were its influences? How did historical empires shape the language and religion? These questions motivate scientists, historians, geographers and anthropologists to travel the world, but I have also found that these sorts of questions underpin my best travel writing.

My questions often emerge from unexpected places – novels, films, or articles in non-travel magazines. They give me a sense of purpose when I go somewhere – a mission to satiate my curiosity – and they help me to frame my journey as I start building an itinerary. Let me give you an example.

A little while ago, I watched a production of the play *The*

Merry Wives of Windsor by William Shakespeare, at a theatre in central London. Back when I was a teenager, there was a pub of that name in Windsor, which never used to ask for ID, so my friends and I used to spend a lot of time there. It's closed now (I don't know if that was due to the lack of ID checks) but it triggered a question of *some* importance: what places in London could I visit that are linked to Shakespeare?

The next step was to find all the different places in London that are mentioned in his plays (fortunately, academics have done all the legwork on this) and then research places in London that were connected with his life. Then I created a walking route to visit them.

It took me to parts of London that I had never been to before – such as Southwark Cathedral, which Shakespeare would have known as St Saviour's – and I got a sense of Shakespeare's London legacy. My curiosity was triggered, and it sent me on a satisfying and enjoyable journey.

Curiosity is the key to travel. It gets us out the door and ensures that we make the most of a place. It needs stimulation to get going but, once the curiosity engine is firing, it wants new questions to answer.

And that's where inspiration comes in.

Chapter 2

INSPIRATION: To Boldly Go

Curiosity is that instinct to peek over the horizon: we have no idea what's out there, but we want to know, so we take a look to find out. Inspiration is curiosity's offspring: we take that peek because someone *else* told us that we might find something interesting.

Inspiration depends on our curious predecessors. They point us in a direction that is likely to reap rewards, and we forge a new path by building on their knowledge. Sir Isaac Newton summed it up by saying, 'if I have seen further, it is by standing on the shoulders of giants.'[13]

Curiosity made the first Polynesian explorers (of Chapter 1) take a look around and discover new islands, then later generations listened to stories about those ancestors, and were inspired to do the same. These successors imagined how they would find and reach more islands, and then they figured out how to do it, by developing new skills and technologies to get there.

Unlike pure curiosity, inspiration depends on the notion of a destination that has already been glimpsed or imagined by someone else. Stories about this destination inspire successors, who create a 'vision' of where they want to get to. That provokes creativity and problem-solving, ranging from the Polynesian boat technology that crossed open oceans, to Newtonian calculations that cross the realms of physics, and even to rockets that can take us to the stars.

When my sister and I were young, Mum ran a bed-and-breakfast in the flat above our family-owned restaurant. Late one night, just as the restaurant was closing, an American named Gael Squibb arrived and asked for a room. His office had booked him into a hotel in Slough, which he had fled after seeing the bathroom.

'Take me somewhere clean!' he had said to the first taxi he came across. The cabbie happened to know Mum and Dad, so he brought the American to us.

Gael worked for the Jet Propulsion Laboratory (JPL), a part of NASA that designs and operates robotic spacecraft, and his work frequently brought him to Britain. He visited our bed-and-breakfast so much that he and his wife, Lee, became close family friends. I have always known them as Uncle Gael and Auntie Lee.

Back in the 1980s, Gael was working on IRAS, an infrared telescope that mapped the heavens. Each JPL mission forged a path that its predecessors had pointed to, with thousands of engineers and scientists developing solutions to difficult problems. But Gael was not just an inspired successor. He was a pioneer, who had joined JPL at the dawn of the Space Age.

'I studied physics at college,' he told me recently. 'My dad said I could always go from physics to engineering, but not the other way round. It turned out to be good advice.'

Gael's strength lay in bridging the needs of scientists – who used the data from instruments in space for research – and the realities of engineers, who had to build and operate the spacecraft that carry those instruments.

'It was an exciting time,' he said, 'and I was part of many "firsts". We didn't look to anyone because nobody had done it before, but that was the exciting part. When you are young, you have this attitude of feeling invincible: maybe you couldn't do it, but you would sure as hell try.

'In 1964, I worked on Surveyor, which conducted the first soft landing on the moon. Before that, a lot of people thought the moon's surface was just a layer of fine dust, which you would sink into on touchdown. That, as you would imagine, was quite a concern for the crewed Apollo landings!'

The early space race repurposed destructive forces for exploration. The rockets that launched the first Russian cosmonaut (Yuri Gagarin) and first American astronaut (Alan Shepard) were converted intercontinental ballistic missiles, designed to deliver nuclear warheads rather than people. And the man behind America's Saturn V moon rocket (Wernher von Braun) had designed the German V2 rockets that bombed London during World War Two.

The inspirational power of space was quickly seized upon by the governments behind it. During the Cold War, the USSR wielded its cosmonauts as proof of communist superiority; the USA's moon landings did the same for American capitalism. And today, NASA's astronauts spend much of their space time on Zoom calls to schoolchildren, encouraging them to take up science (and to support the budget-hungry space programme).

I grew up in an exciting era for space science and technology. In 1989, *Voyager 2* became the first spacecraft to reach the planet Neptune. Four years later, the Hubble Space Telescope was daringly repaired by spacewalking astronauts, so that it could reveal secrets about the birth and death of stars, and by the dawn of the new millennium the International Space Station was being assembled 250 miles above my head. I loved space, so to have an uncle who recounted stories from that pioneering age was deeply inspirational.

'I remember bringing you stuff from JPL's public information office,' Gael said. 'Images of the missions that I'd worked on, and which we were planning – Viking, Ulysses, Voyager – you got all excited, and asked how they worked, and what I did. You wanted to discover things.'

My first dream was to become an astronaut. But, as an overweight asthmatic with bad eyesight, the odds were stacked against me. Luckily, I loved cosmology and astrophysics, so, if I could not explore the universe in person, I was content to do so through the lens of a telescope, or by building the machines that could go there. Now that I had a vision, I just had to figure out how to get there.

Mum let me loose in the library several times a week, where I lost myself in books that imagined the future and explained orbital mechanics. She even took me to a university open day when I was 12 years old, to inspire me with possible science courses. I threw myself into maths and science, and applied to study chemistry and molecular physics at university. I didn't know what job it would get me, but I knew that it was a step closer to my vision of space, and the stories that had inspired me.

The inspiration that launched me towards space was a product of many things: a NASA engineer staying at my parents' bed-and-breakfast; visiting observatories to see the planets for myself; growing up in a time of huge leaps in both manned and robotic space exploration; and being pointed in a direction of study. But at the heart of that inspiration were charismatic personalities, stunning visuals and great storytelling.

So inspiration requires a few things to take off. **Pioneers** are the first curious souls to start exploring a new concept or place. They don't know what the destination will be, but they point their successors in a direction. Then **storytelling** is needed to pass on information and capture the imagination of **successors**, who need to have courage and innovation to overcome the obstacles between themselves and their destination.

In December 2015, the first British astronaut in over a quarter of a century (and the first to be funded by the UK government) arrived at the International Space Station. The UK Space Agency ran an outreach campaign alongside that mission, using space to get people interested in STEM subjects (science, technology, engineering and maths). It was a huge success, with around two million children getting involved, in more than 10,000 schools.[14] The person behind it was Libby Jackson, and today she is the head of space exploration for the UK Space Agency.

'Storytelling got me hooked on space,' she said. 'As a teenager, I read everything about the pioneering years of Apollo. It was just so audacious: humans went from never having been in space, to standing on the moon, in just eight years. Who wouldn't be inspired by that?'

A school physics teacher told Libby about a 'Summer Space School', and she visited a factory in Britain that built satellites.

'That was the moment I realised that "space" was something people did as a job. And not just the stuff of stories.'

Libby wrote a letter to NASA, asking to do some work experience, which is a bit like writing to the English Football Association and asking to shadow the coaching staff of the national team. To her astonishment, they said yes, and she spent two weeks at Mission Control in Houston. After studying physics and astronautics she landed a job in Mission Operations in England, then moved to Germany when the European Space Agency began building the Columbus module of the International Space Station.

'I just searched for jobs and applied,' she said. 'It's incredible how bold and naïve you are in your twenties, but that makes things possible – the average age of the Apollo Flight Controllers was 28. And that boldness worked for me, too: I qualified as a flight director for crewed spaceflight missions at the age of 26 – my dream since I was 17 years old.'

Stories of the Apollo pioneers inspired Libby towards a destination, then determination helped her to reach it. Seven years into her time as a flight director, the UK decided to fund its own astronauts for the first time, and Libby was asked to oversee the public outreach programme. As one of the only other Brits at the European Space Agency, she already knew the man who would become Britain's first official astronaut: Major Tim Peake.

'Space is inspiring because it's different,' Libby said, 'We are just fascinated by it. Things float. You float! You look back down on the Earth – which contains everything that has ever been known and everyone that has ever lived – and you look into the blackness of the sky, with the limitless stars, and you wonder what's out there.

'But it's the human stories that inspire us. For me, it was the pioneering Apollo mission controllers – people like Gene Kranz, Gerry Griffin and Chris Kraft – who solved problems, made decisions, kept the missions going and saved astronauts' lives.'

Libby used the idea of human-centred stories in the outreach programme, and focused on what it was like to live in space. Through the experiences of astronauts, she could then shine a light on the technology and research behind it, from orbital mechanics to thermodynamics, and even to history and geography.

'It's innately human to be curious and want to go somewhere,' she said, 'but without telling the stories of pioneers and successors, we wouldn't know what's possible. It was stories that inspired Ernest Shackleton and James Cook, Ibn Battuta and Ferdinand Magellan. Everybody working on the space programme today discovered it through stories. Without stories, humans would not be going to space.'

For the historian Yuval Noah Harari, the ability to tell stories is a distinctive feature of our species, and the reason we dominate the planet. In his bestselling book *Sapiens,* he explains that many human species (such as Neanderthals and Denisovans) could use tools and fire, and form complex social groups. But only our species, Homo sapiens, went further, inventing everything from boats to commerce within the space of 40,000 years. Harari calls this step the 'Cognitive Revolution', and it depended upon complex language.

Complex language allowed humans to go from saying, 'There's a gazelle over there, let's kill it,' to, 'I saw a gazelle at the watering hole this morning, so if we lay in wait there tomorrow morning, we might be able to ambush it.' That allowed us to plan ahead, and achieve results that far outstripped our comparatively puny physical capabilities. It meant we could gather more resources and survive in otherwise hostile environments.

But, for Harari, the most significant feature of Homo sapiens's language is our ability to talk about things that don't exist in the real world. Harari calls these things 'myths', and they are incredibly powerful because they can be shared. That allows us to cooperate with strangers.

Two English football fans, who have never met, can share a belief in the importance of 11 men, who represent the nation state of 'England' in a game of imagined rules. The game is a myth because it does not exist beyond the collectively shared belief in the rules; and the nation state is a myth, which depends on collectively shared stories about its origin and symbols (such as a flag of white and red).

Collectively shared myths are known as 'social constructs', and they include nation states, corporations, money, democracy, human rights, science, hunting strategies and trade. They are the glue that lets us organise, and which made Homo sapiens different to our predecessors.

Myths depend on stories: a collection of events, strung together in a compelling way, to make the listener believe something. That means stories are deeply bound up in our distinctive competitive advantage. And stories also inspire us to travel.

The Grand Tour was a coming-of-age tradition for British aristocrats in the seventeenth to nineteenth centuries. Inspired by the tales of Christian pilgrims to the Holy Land, the Grand Tourists travelled across Europe, on a route that promised a rich education in art and culture. Many of them wrote about their travels, although these books often feature more tales of drinking and promiscuity than discussions of spiritual revelation.

The era of the Grand Tour came to an end with the Industrial Revolution. Merchants, traders, industrialists and inventors became wealthy. Railways and steamships made travel faster and cheaper. The aristocracy's domination of travel was diluted and, in the 1850s, Thomas Cook (an English businessman who founded a company in his own name) began organising affordable group tours to Europe. Services in the destination countries grew to fill the demand, and mass tourism was born.

In the mid-1950s groups of wealthy Brits breathed new life into the concept of the Grand Tour, and took their vehicles to explore the Silk Road. This series of ancient trade routes linked Europe to Asia via Turkey, Iran and Afghanistan, then onto Pakistan, India and Nepal. The central part of the route crossed deserts and hazardous mountain roads, so these 'Overlanders' had to be self-sufficient, but they also depended on the hospitality of locals in remote settlements. Their rewards were remarkable stories, cultural insights and seeing places that were pseudomythical to most Europeans.

These journeys resonated with devotees of *On the Road,* the 1957 novel by the Beatnik author Jack Kerouac, which follows a young man's quest for meaning and self-expression through a series of motorcar odysseys across America. Fans of the book craved their own formative adventures, and when they heard about the overland route to India they set out to create the ultimate road trip.

Groups of intrepid travellers clubbed together to drive east, and bus companies began operating routes from London or Amsterdam to Delhi or Kathmandu. The journey took around four weeks, and hostels quickly developed along the route. Cafés in Istanbul, Kabul and Peshawar became fabled centres of information, where travellers swapped tips about beaches, gurus, mountain retreats and dope.

Most people who chose to hit the 'Hippy Trail' (as it became known) were inspired by stories from friends who had already done it. Then, in 1968, The Beatles spent a few months at a meditation retreat in India, and their stay was diligently covered by British, American and European media. That introduced the Hippy Trail to a vast new audience.

By the early 1970s, thousands of young Westerners were travelling the route every year. In 1973, Tony and Maureen Wheeler published a 94-page pamphlet, based on their overland journey from London to Sydney; it featured routes, itineraries, places to eat and stay, budgeting advice, cultural and historical insights, information on visas, health and safety tips, maps and personal anecdotes. It was the first *Lonely Planet* guidebook, and was so well trusted by travellers that they referred to it as 'The Bible'.

The curtain fell on the Hippy Trail in 1979, when the Soviet Union invaded Afghanistan and revolution came to Iran, making the overland route near-impossible. Cheap airfares made it possible to fly directly to India or Thailand. The latter became popular during the Vietnam War, when American soldiers used it as a base for logistics and recreation. Vietnam itself opened up to backpackers in the mid-1990s.

Budget travellers clung to *Lonely Planet* as the ultimate authority on what they should see and where they should go, which meant that they all ended up in the same towns and hostels. As traveller numbers grew, and recommended hostels filled up, enterprising locals opened new ones nearby and entire districts turned into backpacker ghettos.

Cafés and restaurants served the same inexpensive foods. Shops sold the same trinkets. Backpackers jumped on the same public buses and hired the same mopeds to visit the same beaches, temples and waterfalls. It wasn't long before the route between Laos, Cambodia, Vietnam and Thailand became known as 'the Banana Pancake Trail', after the favoured food of backpackers.

Alex Garland's novel *The Beach* (1996), about a backpacker discovering a hidden Thai paradise, inspired a new generation to hit the road. When it was made into a film starring Leonardo DiCaprio, backpacker travel – with all its adventure, anxiety, self-discovery and self-destruction – hit the mainstream.

Stories are at the heart of travel inspiration. Each generation goes because of what they have heard from predecessors and pioneers, and the content of those stories shapes how the next generation engages with a place.

As we have seen from Harari, stories are powerful. The stories of the space programme led to new missions, and inspired people to become part of the journey by taking up STEM subjects. Christian pilgrims inspired Grand Tourists, who inspired Silk Road motorists, who (alongside Kerouac) inspired the Hippy Trail, which inspired backpackers.

Whatever the inspiration of the first pioneers, the nature of travel changes with those who follow on. As backpacking progressed, it became less about discovering the place and people, and more about self-discovery and hedonism (something noticeable about *The Beach* is that the main character barely interacts with any of the Thai locals).

As we shall see in later chapters, there's nothing wrong with self-discovery and hedonism as motivations. But it feels like a missed opportunity. It is often said that travel broadens our mind, but is this really true? How can stories inspire us to learn more about the places that we visit?

While I never made it to space, I did the next best thing and visited the Jet Propulsion Laboratory in Pasadena, California. JPL has the most inspiring motto of any public organisation – 'Dare Mighty Things' – and the foyer features a full-size model of Explorer 1, America's very first satellite. The site is an active workshop and, from an observation window overlooking the 'Clean Room', I watched technicians assembling the Curiosity rover that would go on to search for signs of life on Mars. On the wall above it were the mission patches of other JPL probes, assembled in the same room, which had made discoveries that changed our concept of the universe.

My absolute highlight was the Deep Space Network control room, which tracks signals from the NASA spacecraft that roam interplanetary space. The board showed the signals being received from the *Voyager* spacecraft (the first human object to reach interstellar space), which was so far away that the signals took over a day to reach Earth. Watching the board flash – with lights and waves of communication – was as exciting to me as a Taylor Swift concert, or meeting Dwayne 'The Rock' Johnson. I felt intimately connected to inspirational endeavours.

Stories inspire a vision, and we travel to explore that vision. But sometimes, we discover something else.

In early 2015, I had just finished speaking at a travel show when a tall Englishman named Ed Reeves asked me if I fancied visiting Albania to write a travel article. Ed had moved there five years previously to set up a tour company, but I had to admit that Albania wasn't top of my list.

'What about going there to follow in the footsteps of a secret British mission to defeat the Nazis?' he asked.

That got my attention. Popular British war history covers Dunkirk and the Battle of Britain, then jumps to the invasion of Normandy, skipping over several years in the middle. I knew that the British had fought in the Mediterranean, North Africa, the Middle East and Far East; but this was the first time that I'd heard mention of Albania.

In 1943, Albania was under the control of fascist Italy. It sat between the Nazi-occupied territories of Yugoslavia and Greece, which made it an important supply route for the Germans. So when Italy surrendered to the Allies in September 1943, the Nazis took over the occupation of Albania. The British decided to make things difficult.

The British Special Operations Executive began to sabotage and ambush German supply routes, and stirred up trouble through Albanian partisans. Brigadier Edmund 'Trotsky' Davies was parachuted into the village of Bizë to increase the scale of operations, but he and his headquarters were discovered by German troops. They spent two months evading capture, being chased through the mountains in midwinter, and Davies wrote about the experience in a book: *Illyrian Venture*.

Ed had stumbled on Davies' tale while researching hiking trails, and he suggested that we retrace the escape route on foot. The chance to tell this story, from a country that Britons rarely visited, filled me with excitement. I found Davies' book in an archive and read it from cover to cover in a weekend.

After flying to Albania's capital, Tirana, we drove deep into the mountains to reach Bizë. This desolate plateau, ringed by limestone peaks, was empty but for the crumbling remains of a communal farm, and a few shepherds producing goat's cheese in wooden huts.

A café had been rigged up in the wrecked shell of an administrative building, where farmers and old men enjoyed coffee, cigarettes and a clear, colourless liquid in small glasses. They smiled, waved me in and handed me a glass, and I took a swig of the liquor. I found it smooth and fruity, but coughed at the high alcohol content, eliciting laughter from the crowd.

'That's raki,' said Dori, who was guiding us through the mountains. 'Alongside the coffee and cigarettes, it makes up the traditional Balkan breakfast. So not only does it fire you up for today's walk, but you are fully immersing yourself in local culture!'

When Davies and his troops were discovered, they fled over a pass into the Gurakuq Valley. You might imagine that they travelled light, but they had enough time to load their donkeys with essential supplies, including the Olivetti typewriter that they used for record-keeping. We followed their route to a former partisan safehouse, where Davies overcame his love of bureaucracy and decided to dump the typewriter. It's still there today.

The next morning we headed towards a pinnacle of rock in which the partisans had hidden a printing press and headquarters. Just before we reached this hiding place, our mule-handler, Rushdi, quietly led us to a clump of trees.

'My family were partisans,' he said. 'My grandfather and great-uncle were interrogated by the Germans, then killed on this spot when they refused to give up the location of the printing press. Their bodies were hung from those trees as a warning.'

Rushdi took the reins of his mule and we followed him to that precious location in a landscape of shattered limestone. A narrow cleft led between two columns of rock, and we climbed a natural staircase. In a depression, protected on three sides by tall chalk walls, was the entrance to a cave, which could only be accessed by sliding through a crack. No wonder the Germans never found it – you could walk within five feet of it and never know it was there. I peeked inside, but the roof had collapsed, burying whatever remained.

We came across the camp of some beekeepers, who had just transported their beehives up the mountain for the summer. One of them handed me a chunk of bread dipped in honey.

'It's nice and mellow,' I said, 'with a smoky woodiness.'

'That's because it was made down in the valley,' he replied, 'with pollen gathered from chestnut trees. Now try this.'

He pulled a frame from a hive, and carefully cut out a square from the honeycomb. These were the first drops of honey from the high alpine meadows, where the bees were collecting pollen from wildflowers rather than trees. I put my lips to the beeswax and sucked. The honey was light and citrusy; completely different to the chestnut batch that the very same bees had produced just a few weeks earlier.

The next morning we began our trek to where Davies' story had ended, in a landscape that wouldn't have looked out of place in Sardinia or Greece. We stopped at a shop for supplies, but they had run out of what we needed, so the young man behind the counter jumped on his bike to get some more.

Five minutes later, he handed us vegetables from his

parents' garden, some fresh bread, and olive oil from a farm in Crete where he'd worked over the summer. He insisted that we take them as gifts.

'We never have tourists here,' he said, 'and I want you to like it.'

We walked beside a cold river, towards the head of the valley, where a steep incline brought us to the hedges of Kostenjë. The village is totally inaccessible to vehicles, so farming hasn't changed for centuries, and three children waved as they passed us on a donkey; they were on their way to a village beyond the mountain pass, and the donkey was their school bus.

While asking for directions, we met a woman whose family had hidden a British soldier during the war. After the war had ended, the family had invited him back for a wedding, but Albania's post-war communist regime wouldn't allow it.

'It's funny,' said her husband, as he handed me some raki. 'We were allies all that time ago. Then during the regime we were enemies. Now we are friends again!'

An hour later, in a remote field high above Kostenjë, we found a sheep-pen. This was meant to be another partisan safehouse for Davies and his troops, with partisan scouts supposedly watching the valley below. But on the morning of 8 January 1944, Davies got word that Albanian collaborators, led by Germans, were in Kostenjë. The scouts had failed them.

Now numbering just six, and surrounded on three sides, the British climbed single file through deep snow to escape. Davies was shot twice and rolled down the slope; after re-covering from his wounds he was taken to the Colditz prisoner of war camp in Germany. He was captured just six miles, as the crow flies, from where he had started in Bizë.

*

Discovery is an essential part of travel, but if we just follow itineraries (where everything has been mapped out and listed in a guidebook) that discovery can feel hollow. We only have to look at the blight of over-tourism at attractions like Barcelona's Park Güell (which has shifted from being a public space to a ticketed tourist site) or Paris's Louvre museum (where it's impossible to see some paintings for the crowds) to realise that copying others can lead to dissatisfying travel experiences.

A relative of inspiration is 'aspiration'. Whereas inspiration leads us to discovery and insight, *aspiration* is about trying to replicate something that someone else has done. Of course, many destinations become popular because they *are* remarkable: the Taj Mahal really is spectacular; Parisian cafés really are lovely; and no two travel experiences will be identical. But my research into inspiration and stories suggests that travelling with a sense of purpose and discovery can be more rewarding than just replicating others' experiences.

Perhaps this is the difference between 'explorers', 'travellers' and 'tourists'. The *explorers* are the **curious** pioneers, who go somewhere that no one has visited before (at least from within the explorer's society or culture). *Travellers* are **inspired** by the pioneers' stories to discover more. And *tourists* then **aspire** to replicate travellers' experiences, through a well-worn path of sanitised discovery.

These are not clear distinctions or definitions, and they overlap in time, or even within an individual. Travellers and explorers can be tourists, too, and I find it wearisome when people try to establish a hierarchy, or to insist that one form of travel is superior to another. Tourism is enjoyable, and we can all make our travels a bit more fulfilling by drawing on the principles of inspiration.

41

The simplest form of inspiration is to visit somewhere that is connected to a person that fascinates you. An American friend of mine likes to visit buildings that David Bowie lived in, and he loves to photograph Banksy's street art. He knows that he's not going to have the same experiences as Bowie, nor meet Banksy, but they give him a reason to visit somewhere new; he's now been to Bristol, Brixton, Berlin and Bethlehem, just to follow in the footsteps of his heroes.

Inspiration can take us to unexpected destinations. The story of the space programme inspired me to study science, but when I got to university I realised that I wanted to understand the questions that *underpin* science, so I switched to studying philosophy.

My travels follow a similar evolution: I begin planning trips because I've been inspired by a particular story or interest, but I end up exploring or experiencing something different. I followed Trotsky Davies because I was interested in the Special Operations Executive, but I discovered a country and culture that was both beautiful and welcoming. It became one of the most rewarding journeys of my life, and I have raved about Albania ever since.

Stories inspire good travel, and, when we build our journeys around them, it can lead to a sense of discovery. But sometimes, we just want a bit of fun.

Chapter 3

HAPPINESS: A Slippery Slope

When I arrived at university, a common getting-to-know-you question was 'do you ski?'[15]. I didn't, but I wanted to, and one of my new friends remembered this. So, when he was planning a skiing holiday to France, he kindly invited me along.

I've never been particularly athletic, so I signed up for some lessons and spent the first few days with my face in the snow. But the moment I first linked my turns together was revelatory. I could control my speed and choose where to go. I could even stop (most of the time), so, on the third afternoon, I took a cable car up the mountain.

If you have never been skiing, let me describe it to you. You travel to a hostile environment, buy clothing that you will never use anywhere else, stick your feet into painful boots and strap a plank of wood onto each foot. You then haul yourself to the top of this dangerous environment (where people have used

---

[15] University was as much an education in social differences, as it was an education in Philosophy.

dynamite to prevent avalanches), then use the planks of wood to slide across layers of frozen water, which hides jagged rocks. At the same time, hundreds of other people, who are barely in control of themselves, descend past you at high speed.

This is, obviously, a ridiculous thing to do. It is expensive, dangerous, and both frustrating and painful to learn. But at the top of the cable car, I suddenly understood why people choose to do it. And I discovered that I love it.

Being *among* the mountains is very different to looking *at* the mountains. The white sea of snow-covered rock rolls away from you, plunging over cliffs, and soaring to jagged peaks; the sky seems closer, and richer in colour; chairlifts chug up impossibly steep slopes, and skiers look like ants, descending the pistes with sprays of snow. The only sound that you can hear is the hiss of skis and people whooping with joy.

After three days on the narrow nursery slope at the bottom of the mountain, the sense of exposure at the top was over-whelming. I followed my friends down the piste – which was wider and steeper than anything I had been on previously – and I let my skis run straight down the hill. The rush of snow beneath my feet, and the force pushing my body as I turned, was extraordinary. I felt a sense of exhilaration and satisfaction, which seemed to last for ever. Until it turned into alarm.

I fought to turn my feet, but it needed more force than I could handle. I caught an edge and continued on one ski, momentarily thinking that I could recover, before I tumbled into an orange crash barrier and my skis detached from my boots. My heart raced and hands shook as I gathered my goggles and gloves and clambered back into the ski-bindings. The fusion of terror, concentration and joy was compelling, and I wanted to find it again. For the rest of the week, I took the first ski-lifts of the day and skied until the mountain closed.

Ski resorts excel at simpler fun, too, in the tradition of après-ski. Bars halfway up the mountain serve pitchers of beer on huge terraces, where DJs mix dance music, and live bands play cover songs. Dancing in ski boots takes practice, particularly when the bar staff pour spirits into your mouth along a ski. The booze is a mixed blessing for the journey back into town: you ski better when you're relaxed, but the slopes look like a bowling alley, with après-skiers scattered like skittles.

During our nights out, I discovered that English people work in French ski resorts – running chalets, working in bars, and even teaching skiing. This was a revelation to me, and by the end of the week I knew that I wanted to spend a season in a ski resort. After university, I did five months of bar work in the French resort of Meribel, then I moved to New Zealand and trained as a ski instructor. That got me a job at a ski school in Verbier, Switzerland, where I mostly shepherded kids down the nursery slopes and into cafés for hot chocolates.

I eventually ended up running a chalet for a wealthy British family, but I had plenty of time between their holidays to train and teach skiing. The active lifestyle and daily après-ski was an enjoyable mix, and there was a constant flow of new tourists and seasonal workers to have fun with. I returned on and off for another six winters because it made me happy.

Ancient Greek philosophers identified two sources of happiness: eudaimonia comes from self-realisation, having a purpose and doing the moral thing; hedonism is the pursuit of pleasure and the avoidance of pain. Eudaimonia is not superior to hedonism – and research suggests that we need both to feel content in life – but hedonistic pleasures tend to be more intense, short-lived and escapist, while eudemonic contentment is more enduring.

Modern psychologists believe that this maps onto some of our motivations for travel. Eudemonic travel seeks personal development through volunteering, learning languages or cultural activities. Hedonistic travel pursues pleasure through good food, fine wine and physical activities; it avoids pain through relaxation and lie-ins.

Ski holidays are a mix of hedonism and eudaimonia because they provide both pleasure and personal development. Some holidays, however, are purely hedonistic.

Ibiza is the world's apex party island, and when I first went there in 2011 – at the recommendation of a DJ who spent his winters in Verbier – it was the most desirable destination in Europe. Ibiza was a byword for glamour, glitz and indulgence. Celebrities wanted to be seen there, and everyone else wanted to see them.

The Phoenicians settled the island in 650 BCE, and named it for Bes, their god of dance and protection. It's an appropriate namesake. Many people know of Ibiza's association with dance music, but the island has always offered protection for the persecuted, too: Jews escaping the Catholic Inquisition, Americans avoiding the Vietnam draft, and liberals fleeing the fascist Franco regime of Spain.

In his book *The White Island,* Stephen Armstrong reveals that Ibiza was a popular place for Roman legionaries to relax, but when it opened to modern tourism in 1959 it was something of a backwater. Many villas and farmhouses had been abandoned during the decades of civil war, so the black-dressed Ibizan locals – who were mostly peasant farmers and salt traders – were grateful for the arrival of opportunity and hard currency.

Ibiza's tourism transformation – from subsistence to super-power – is worth understanding, because it is the first destination to have gone through the entire evolution, and it is a model that has been replicated across the world, for good and for ill.

Franco opened Spain to tourism as a way to boost its economy, and Armstrong's research suggests that the first tourists to Ibiza were Dutch artists and writers, who encouraged their bohemian and jazz musician friends to travel down from Paris. They were followed by actors from all over the world, many of whom bought homes in the countryside, as well as American draft-dodgers who settled in Ibiza Old Town. The draft-dodgers had con-nections with Europe's hippy communities, who rented deserted farmhouses and organised huge free parties.

My friend Bridget Mills-Powell first went to Ibiza at least a decade before I did. She worked there for a season after school and went on to become a journalist at the dance-culture maga-zine *Mixmag*. While writing for them she spent much of her time in Ibiza, reporting on the latest developments in dance music.

'Ibiza allowed people to fulfil all of their wants and desires,' she told me. 'But it also provided a sense of community, and a place for everyone to be themselves.'

Ibiza's cultural tolerance meant that it developed a vibrant gay scene, and this heady mix of fun-seekers led to Ibiza's first nightclubs, including Pacha and Amnesia. Rock stars like Frank Zappa and Queen's Roger Taylor got in on the vibe and bought houses on the island. Pink Floyd set up a studio, while James Brown, Freddie Mercury and Tina Turner all performed at Ku nightclub.

'Ibiza transformed the way music was consumed,' Bridget

said. 'Back in the 1970s and 1980s, most clubs played a specific genre of music, but the clubs in Ibiza played a mix of disco, pop and funk – whatever got the crowd going. The super-clubs could hold up to 10,000 people, with huge performances and stage shows, so it was like a festival every night. Nowhere else in the world did anything like that.

'But the big transformation was the arrival of dance music. The popular legend – and it seems to be true – is that an Argentinian DJ called Alfredo, brought Chicago House to Ibiza in 1985. He mixed it with pop music, like Prince and Tears for Fears, in a style that became known as "Balearic Beat".'

The final piece of the puzzle was ecstasy. Ibiza was not the first place to see people taking the drug for fun – clubbers in America had been using it for a few years – but its arrival on the island coincided with the development of Alfredo's Balearic Beat. According to Stephen Armstrong, MDMA[16] came to Ibiza with a spiritual cult and, from there, it spread to the nightclubs. What nobody could have predicted was the impact that it would have on Britain.

Upper-class Brits leaving colonial service had been settling in Ibiza since the 1960s, but the big British influx came with the arrival of package holidays and cheap airfares. By the 1980s, the town of San Antonio had become a playground of beer-swilling hooligans, until, in 1987, four London music-heads went to Ibiza to celebrate a birthday, and changed British music for ever.

Danny Rampling, Paul Oakenfold, Nicky Holloway and Johnny Walker swallowed a load of ecstasy, went to watch

---

[16] The active component of ecstasy.

Alfredo play at Amnesia, and had the best night of their lives. Inspired to emulate DJ Alfredo's Balearic Beat, Rampling founded the club night 'Shoom' near London Bridge. Oakenfold established 'Future' at Heaven, and Holloway set up 'The Trip' at Astoria. Acid House was born.

Ecstasy arrived in Britain at around the same time, and this convergence of events led to the 'second summer of love' in 1988. People have credited it with everything from ending Thatcherism to reducing football hooliganism, although there were plenty of other social changes going on in Britain at the same time. Either way, it was a cultural moment for a disenfranchised generation, who flooded to nightclubs in record numbers.

Ibiza became *the* destination for music fans, who went for the great weather, incredible stage shows and world-renowned DJs. The glamour, celebrities and sunshine drew music journalists, TV documentaries and ever-more tourists, whose numbers grew from 40,000 a year in the 1960s to several hundred thousand a year in the 1980s. By the time I arrived in 2011, Ibiza was receiving over 3 million visitors annually.

It felt like it. There was barely a spot on the beach at Playa d'en Bossa, and every inch of the shoreline was covered with multistorey hotels and apartment buildings. But there was still a whiff of Ibiza's legendary generosity in the air.

A mate had gone out there before me and got chatting to a promotional rep for one of the clubs. Ally Renfrew was one of many Brits who had gone to Ibiza on holiday and chosen to stay, and she let us sleep on her sofa (which was far nicer than the warren-like hotels nearby).

'Well, it beats Glasgow,' she said, 'but there's something magical about Ibiza – it pulls at you like a magnet. Everyone's so friendly, there's amazing music every night, and the weather's fantastic. What's not to like?'

She went on to tell me that Ibiza has ley lines of spiritual power running through it, connecting it to sites like Stonehenge. The offshore pinnacle of Es Vedrà is supposed to be the tip of Atlantis, and the sacred spirit of the island is the goddess Tanit, whom the Phoenicians allegedly worshipped with sacred orgies.

Ally had arranged free tickets to Space, one of the biggest and most renowned super-clubs in the world. The queue was a carnival, with people dressed in feathers, bikinis and bondage gear, and the music in the main arena was more than just sound – it was the very air. The whole audience was moving as one, rather than bouncing around individually, and I was immediately swept up by the euphoria, gazing up at lasers that beamed patterns into clouds of dry ice.

After hours of non-stop dancing, I was thirsty. Bottles of water were €15, and the tap water in the toilets was deliberately salty, so I stumped up the €18 for a beer, happy that Ally had saved us €60 each on our tickets. Dutch, French, Swedish and American clubbers all crossed our path, and chatted about everything and nothing. By the end of the night, I had dozens of new friends.

We stumbled out into the dawn light and headed for the nearest hilltop. As the sun breached the horizon, we threw our arms around each other, marvelling at something that happened every single day but which had never seemed so glorious. After half an hour we all wandered off in different directions, and I slept on Ally's sofa until sunset.

That evening I had arranged to meet Rob (the DJ from Verbier), who was hosting a party on a yacht. He told me that

I'd know it when I saw it, but one massive white yacht looks much like another when you are wandering around a marina of thousands. Eventually I spotted some purple lasers flashing from a boat as big as an airliner, and wandered towards it.

At the bottom of a gangplank stood a tall blond woman dressed like an air hostess. I looked down at my pink shorts, grey polo shirt and shabby trainers, and realised that I should have asked Rob about the dress code for yacht parties.

The hostess checked my name against a list and handed me a glass of champagne. Then she unhooked a velvet rope so that I could toddle up the rocking, red-carpeted gangplank, spilling my champagne as I went.

At the top was a vast desk, surrounded by white cushioned sofas that were occupied by middle-aged men dressed in white linen and gold watches. Groups of women danced in groups, apart from five or six who were splashing around in a hot tub. A man in leather chaps skipped around the dance-floor, breathing fire in time to the music, while hostesses handed out plates of sushi.

Rob spotted me standing there with my mouth open, and waved me over to the DJ booth.

'Glad you could make it,' he said. 'A bit different to your usual nightlife, I guess?'

The fire-breather finished his set to rapturous applause, and the dance-floor started to fill up. A few minutes later, Rob introduced me to someone who was standing nearby.

'So what do you do on the island?' I asked.

'I'm a DJ,' he replied.

'Oh, cool,' I said. 'Just on the yachts, or do you work at any of the bars on the island?'

'Uh, yeah. I actually have a residency at Space.'

51

I didn't know a lot about dance music, but I knew that a residency at Space was one of the most coveted gigs on the planet, like an actor winning an Oscar and then getting every film role that they wanted for the rest of their career. Whoever I was speaking to, they must have been good at what they did.

'Who was that?' I asked Rob, after the other DJ had shuffled off.

'DJ Sasha,' he said.

Sasha was one of the biggest names in dance music. Having grown up in Wales, he took up DJ'ing just as the UK clubbing scene exploded, and went on to play at every venue worth mentioning. He was the world's first superstar DJ and produced music for the world's biggest pop stars, but he also achieved critical acclaim, winning a Grammy award along the way.

'Oh,' I replied, 'I just asked him if he only played on yachts.'

'Cool move,' said Rob. 'That's like asking Madonna if she's a wedding singer.'

Once Rob had finished his set, we wandered towards the Old Town. He had been coming to Ibiza since he was in his twenties, and had been working there for a dozen summers.

'It's a real cliché,' he said, 'but it's changed. From somewhere that was word-of-mouth, to somewhere that everyone knows about. By the time I started coming, Brits were heading to the clubs, and not just getting wasted in San Antonio. That's probably a good thing, but the growth in numbers is hard to get your head around.'

'Did that change things?' I asked.

'Like you wouldn't believe,' said Rob. 'Buildings started going up everywhere, and planning depended on who you knew. Misbehaviour that had been limited to San Antonio spread all over the island, which upset locals – I mean, would you want a bunch of wasted Geordies fighting and pissing on your doorstep?'

When the island first opened to tourism, San Antonio was a fishing village, and the island's main town (also, confusingly, called Ibiza) was just a fort, harbour, market and cafés. Today, Ibiza Old Town is full of designer shops, where the ultra-rich take a shopping break from their yachts.

'The wealthy and glamorous always came to Ibiza,' Rob said. 'But it wasn't always so divided. Even if the rich retreated to their villas to sleep, everyone was in the clubs together, and there was only a limited number of bars and restaurants.

'Today, there's thousands of yachts parked up in the marina and thousands of top-end villas. The proportion of wealthy people is probably the same as ever, but it's much more in-your-face. There are more tourists overall, and places have opened to cater exclusively to the rich. It's a different kind of wealth, too. More showy.'

Increased demand for accommodation, and the sheer volume of tourists, has made Ibiza more expensive. It is becoming unaffordable for many, including seasonal workers, and that's changing the culture of the island: budget travellers and ravers are being replaced with older, wealthier tourists.

But not everyone is unhappy with this shift. The old hotels, built for large numbers of budget holidaymakers, swallowed up land in prime locations, while their pools and facilities strained water supplies on an already dry island. And with most of the hotels being all-inclusive, visitors did not put much money back into the rest of the local economy. A switch to fewer, higher-spending tourists feels more sustainable to many locals.

Ibiza finds itself in a tricky situation. The arrival of tourism changed the fortunes of its inhabitants, some of whom went from subsistence farming to jet-setting in just two generations. But with 95 per cent of Ibiza's economic output related to tourism, it has created a dependency that was disastrous during the pandemic, and which has led to resentment among some locals.

'Think about it,' said Rob. 'If you grew up watching your parents cater to pissed-up Brits and bossy rich Russians, would you want to stay here? Many Ibizans with ambitions beyond tourism head to the mainland for work.'

Ibiza's tourist board has made a conscious effort to change the island's image and look after the interests of locals. The nightclubs were forced to build roofs over their open-air dance floors in the 1990s, and they are constantly fighting legal challenges over noise and crowd sizes. Space shut down in 2016 and turned into a restaurant, and Amnesia closed during the pandemic. The music scene has evolved, too, with Instagram-conscious partygoers favouring glitzy spots like Ocean Beach Club over the sweat-pits of the super-clubs.

'Maybe it's just not my place any more,' said Rob. 'But that's fine. Most of my peers and friends have moved on to other things and different lives. I'm twice the age of most of the tourists coming here – which was the age *I* was when I discovered Ibiza. Things change. But we change, too. Maybe different things make me happy now.'

In *The Psychology of Travel*,[17] Dr Andrew Stevenson explores an idea by Dr Daisy Fan, which categorises tourists by how much (or little) they interact with locals:

'*Dependents*' travel with friends or relatives on package tours. They avoid interaction with locals wherever possible and stick to resorts or guided sightseeing.

'*Conservatives*' speak to locals for information, but rarely beyond those who work in tourism, like hotel staff, tour guides or taxi drivers.

'*Criticisers*' are more experienced travellers who do independent sightseeing, but only on well-trodden paths.

'*Explorers*' (in Dr Fan's model) go out of their way to engage with locals, to learn about their lives so that their preconceptions can be challenged. They make a deliberate effort to visit places that are not on the tourist trail.

'*Belonging-seekers*' participate in the lives of locals, developing friendships for their own sake and not just for information. Where possible, they will live with locals, and often extend the duration of their stay.

Dr Fan's scale moves from zero decision-making as a 'dependent' to total responsibility as a 'belonging-seeker'. Dependents have a tour operator to plan their itinerary, fix any problems and organise their hotel and transport, while the belonging-seeker is on their own. Autonomy can bring great rewards (including the dopamine kick of curious discovery), but it takes time to build up the skills, confidence and judgement that we need for independent travel.

In my experience, travelling in a group reduced my decision-making and gave me a sense of security, which allowed me to develop the skills that I needed for independent travel. When I went on the rugby tour to New Zealand, I was a 'dependent' within a group, until conversations with Kiwis challenged my preconceptions, and pushed me into the mode of an 'explorer'.

But I have also found that I can move in both directions along the scale. After I finished school (about a year after the rugby tour) I spent three months travelling around India, to learn more about my heritage on my father's side. I started with a week at my uncle's house in Delhi, where I spent my time visiting relatives, temples and weddings, and I even went on a pilgrimage with my cousin. I fitted into the category of 'belonging-seeker'. But when I began travelling the country on my own, things started to change.

My first stop was the city of Agra, which is the home of the Taj Mahal and one of India's busiest tourist destinations. It's chaotic, and has a reputation for conmen exploiting naïve tourists. With my sense of security challenged, I fell in with a group of other backpackers and took their advice, rather than that of the 'untrustworthy' locals. I focused on seeing the sights, rather than engaging with local culture, which made me a 'criticiser'.

I travelled with members of that group for about a week, then left them as I moved on to quieter places. I realised that I had become dependent on them (or *Lonely Planet*) for all of my decisions, and that I was isolating myself from my surroundings. So I began making an effort to ask locals about what I should see and do. By the time I made it to the city of Varanasi, I felt more confident and secure in my abilities. I spent most of my time there with the family who owned the guesthouse that I stayed in, and barely spoke to any other backpackers.

This does not mean that one mode of travel is better than the other. Sometimes we only want to decide which cocktail to drink, or what time to eat, in which case a package holiday is perfect. Sometimes we just want to have fun, rather than learning about the history and culture of a place. It all depends on what makes us happy at the time.

My ski holiday was hedonistic with a touch of eudemonia,

but Ibiza was purely hedonistic. I was not in a tour group for either of them, but the only locals I spoke to were the ski instructor in France, and the off-licence owner in Ibiza. I was one of Dr Fan's 'dependents'.

Ski resorts in Europe are fairly content with their model of 'dependent' foreign tourists because new development is limited, and everyone has to pay for a ski pass. Both the buildings and pistes are on land owned by local farmers, who make a fortune from fields that are otherwise useless during winter. But Ibiza is trying to shift its market from dependent hedonists to eudemonic explorers, and there are good reasons to do so.

The evolution of Ibiza has been repeated all over the world, in places ranging from Bali to Thailand, and from the Masai Mara to Montmartre. Paul Fotsch, a professor of globalisation, describes this template as 'standardisation, commodification and historical distortion,'[18] but it is more popularly known as 'Disney-fication'. When we combine it with Dr Fan's model, it starts to make sense.

For a few years or decades, a place is only known to belonging-seekers and explorers, who are interested in the rich and appealing culture, history and landscape of somewhere off the beaten track. They visit the place for its own merits, and bring income and opportunities to a deprived region. Then word-of-mouth reaches criticisers, who seek novelty but demand familiar accommodation and services, with a veneer of the host culture on top. Locals make the most of that market appeal and replicate the buildings, institutions and events that tourists want, 'standardising' the whole place.

The place's original culture (which drew tourists in the first place) fades from consciousness, and the community and heritage becomes 'commodified', as operators sell an *idea* of the place instead of its underlying truth. Operators organise direct flights and package holidays for conservatives and dependents, who want low-cost cookie-cutter holidays and familiar brands. As the economy transforms, it shifts to servicing the needs of tourists, rather than locals, with souvenir shops and cafés replacing local stores. The most marketable aspects of the culture might even be copied and exported, so the place's uniqueness becomes lost or diluted.

Finally, the history of the place is 'distorted'. It's not deliberately falsified, but it gets simplified, romanticised and selectively edited as the original culture is lost. Eventually, only the myth remains.

That's what I found in Ibiza: an appealing narrative of hedonism and self-actualisation, drawing on the myth of a culture that, actually, no longer exists. Critically, for places like Ibiza, it's the myth about the experience of *former tourists* that draws in the next generation of visitors. The stories and culture of people *from* Ibiza are largely absent from the narrative.

That's not to deny that it's compelling. While I was in Ibiza, I hung out on beaches, listened to DJs and enjoyed the weather. I could have found a version of that on dozens of Mediterranean islands (most of which have commodified and imported the club-and-beach culture of Ibiza), but it was the myth about Ibiza's heritage that made it so fulfilling.

Mass-market tourism focuses on the hedonistic because it's easier to sell and package. FUN! RELAXATION! NO DECISIONS! DRINK THIS! EAT THAT! The extreme version is cruise holidays, where tourists move around on devastatingly polluting ships, cocooned in a familiar world, with other tourists. They stop at a harbour, sightsee with a ship's guide, and visit souvenir shops and restaurants that have a deal with the cruise company. Barely any money reaches the local economy, and the tourists never meet a local.

While exploiting myths and hedonism can have damaging consequences for cultures and the environment, it can be even worse when capitalism leverages eudemonic intentions.

The film *The Last Tourist* (2021) reveals how the myth of volunteering has had devastating effects in some countries. Volunteering in the developing world started with Christian missionaries, who gave locals education and medicine in exchange for their devotion. Events like the famine in 1980s Ethiopia led to charities like Live Aid and Comic Relief raising money for good causes. The fundraisers or celebrity ambassadors then went out to see how the money had helped, and maybe lend a hand with the work while they were there.

The photos of these fundraisers (usually white) with the recipients of their aid (usually children of colour) inspired a desire in others to do the same thing, often out of good intentions. 'Voluntourism' developed as way to commodify this, where tourists pay to volunteer for a couple of weeks; it is now one of the fastest growing trends in tourism and generates around $2 billion of revenue a year.[19]

This can provide vital funding to legitimate organisations. But it has also, perversely, incentivised the wrong type of outcomes in desperately poor regions of Africa and Asia.

From 2005 until 2022, there was a 75 per cent increase in the number of orphanages in Cambodia,[20] which matches the growth in voluntourism; but around 80 per cent of the children in these orphanages still have at least one parent.[21] 'Child finders' capitalise on parents' concerns about poverty and persuade them to hand over their children, with the promise of education and accommodation.[22] But most of the money raised from volun-tourists goes to the orphanage owners, rather than the communities, families or children who need it.

The children live in crowded dormitories in dreadful conditions, while there are no qualifications checks for the paying volun-tourists, who usually have no idea how to teach.

'Imagine a busload of tourists coming into a school and disturbing the class,' says Clarissa Elakis of ChildSafe International in *The Last Tourist*. 'They play with the kids, take selfies with them, give out candy, and expect the kids to do a performance for them. Would this happen in your home country? Probably not. So why do tourists think it's okay to do it in developing countries?'

These children are not in these orphanages because they *need* to be there, but because tourists *want* them to be there. The industry is driving the removal of children from families. The tourists leave with their photos and a sense of having done some good, while the kids are left with a poor education, attachment issues and deep trauma. Their rates of suicide are much higher than in the rest of the country, and when they leave these business-orphanages they are much more vulnerable to sex trafficking and other forms of criminal exploitation.

The same model leads to wild animals being captured (or bred) and abused, so that tourists can be photographed with them. The eudemonic motivation of these tourists – to help deprived people, or to love animals – is admirable, but it is being abused by crooks.

This chapter has laid out a grim roll call: the commodification and erosion of communities; habitat destruction through overdevelopment; and the exploitation of vulnerable children and animals. Does this mean that we need to give up on tourism altogether?

Not necessarily. Problems occur when we view people and places as resources for our happiness. We package them into a myth, which we consume to give us pleasure, or to make us feel good about ourselves.

There's nothing wrong with hedonistic or eudemonic tourism, but there are ways to do it better. I believe that Dr Daisy Fan's model is an excellent guiding compass, which not only reduces the harm that tourists can cause but can actually take our travel experience to the next level.

Hedonism (including rest and relaxation) is a perfectly legitimate reason to travel. It's the reason that most of us will travel, most of the time. But the places we visit are the homes of the people who look after us, and we must treat both with respect. Are we genuinely interested in locals' lives and cultures, or are we commodifying them?

An explorer or belonging-seeker can have a relaxing and hedonistic beach holiday. The key is to engage with local people – rather than just seeing them as resources – and that starts with accommodation. The original format of Airbnb matched visitors with locals' spare rooms, or airbeds on their living room floor. It gave locals some extra cash, and gave visitors insider advice on a destination.

As Airbnb grew, landlords began renting out entire flats (that would otherwise be people's homes), pushing up rental prices for residents. Visitors no longer interacted with their hosts, and in popular areas – Cornwall, the Lake District, Amsterdam – locals moved out due to the lack of affordable housing, and local shops shifted to serving tourists instead.

That's bad for locals, and dissatisfying for visitors, because they experience a Disneyfied, sanitised version of a place. This gap between expectation and reality is explored in Woody

Allen's film *Midnight in Paris* (2011). The lead character realises that everyone hankers after a myth that they will never be able to access, and there's always a sense that 'it used to be better'. We can see this playing out in places like Ibiza, but within that lies an opportunity: to be the explorer of somewhere new, rather than the dependent going somewhere well-trodden.

That said, it's still possible to visit popular places without feeling like the meat in a tourist sausage-factory. On a recent trip to Montmartre – the Parisian hill that is home to the Sacré-Cœur cathedral – I enjoyed the excellent view of the city alongside hundreds of other tourists, but then I dodged the nearby street of copy-paste restaurants that had menus in a dozen languages. On the advice of a friend who lived in Paris, I headed north, wandered down a staircase into the 18th arrondissement, and left the tourist-flooded streets behind. A few blocks down, I found Co18, where a band played jazz on the pavement, and locals chatted to me about the changing nature of Paris. It was magical, and the type of relaxed encounter that I had presumed impossible in the busiest tourist city in the world.

If you're in search of fulfilling hedonistic travel, follow the mindset of the explorer and get off the beaten track. Eat local food; it is a window into the culture and prevents the creep of standardisation. Drink wine from the country you're in (and, if they don't produce wine, they probably serve beer).[23] Think about where you stay; hosted accommodation in people's homes (which puts money directly back into the local com-

---

[23] This also reduces carbon emissions, by reducing the demand for food and drink imported from abroad.

munity) still exists if you spend the time looking for it, and if you want your own space you can stay in a locally owned guesthouse, rather than corporate-owned hotels. You can also ask the owners of the guesthouse about their country, and what places they recommend visiting – it's the easiest path to that most delightful of holiday outcomes: good memories.

For eudemonic tourism, question whether your activity is genuinely helping people (or animals) or just making you feel good about yourself. If you are paying to perform a task that you'd expect a professional to do back home (like teaching kids) you are probably doing more harm than good. Instead, take what you're already good at, and use that to help. A social media whizz, accountant, chef or solicitor can spend a few months giving an organisation invaluable expertise (much more valuable than teaching dodgy English lessons), and you can find audited charities through World Animal Protection and ChildSafe International.

The market is also making a dent in exploitative practices, as wised-up tourists demand that their money does some good. G Adventures and Explore Travel champion initiatives that put money back into the local economy, even in places as well-trodden as Machu Picchu and Mt Kilimanjaro. Exodus Travels works with researchers on its adventure holidays, so that paying guests can do citizen science that protects the places they visit. And Intrepid Travel places indigenous-owned tourism at the centre of its business model, putting money straight into communities and at-risk habitats.

'As tour operators,' says Bruce Poon Tip of G Adventures, 'we have to create a dialogue with the local community, and listen to what local people want. That's the magic of tourism: when you get it right, you meet the needs of everyone.'

So even as a short-term tourist, we can make choices that help a place, rather than harm it. Moving to a country, as either a seasonal or long-term worker, can have an even bigger impact. The whole point of travel is to see new places and learn new things, but it's easy to just spend our time with people just like us – other long-term tourists. Once again, the answer is to move back up Dr Fan's scale of local engagement.

A good friend of mine, Tom Waddington, runs a ski school in Verbier, which is staffed by British instructors, and caters to British tourists; but he also speaks fluent French and volunteers for the local fire service. Tom doesn't just take from the region; he gives back with his time, his effort, and at the risk of his own life. He never imagined that following his hedonistic love of skiing could be so eudaimonically rewarding, but he has made Verbier his home, and is probably the most content seasonal worker I know.

So, we can still pursue happiness – whether hedonistic or eudemonic – and we can do it without damaging the people or places we visit. We just need to think about what we are doing. But hedonism can also be an avenue to more fulfilling travel, in the vein of Dr Fan's 'explorers'.

Theatre runs in the blood of my friend Libby Brodie – her brother is an actor and her parents actually met at drama school – and she always knew that she wanted to work in theatre production. When I first got to know her, Libby was working at the Old Vic theatre in London, and we bonded over a shared love of Shakespeare and wine. She eventually established a production company of her own, putting on plays like *Madagascar The Musical*, but, when Covid lockdowns devastated the theatre industry, all of her work was put on hold.

'My company folded overnight,' she told me. 'So I took to drink and then accidentally monetised it.'

Libby decided to do an online course with the Wine & Spirit Education Trust, to gain a deeper appreciation of her favourite tipple.

'When I started the course,' she said, 'I just wanted to learn about wine, and I had the naïve arrogance of ignorance, which meant that I would ask basic questions, rather than being intimidated. So when I talk about wine to other people, I use the language that made sense to me as a beginner.'

Libby began posting anonymous wine reviews on Instagram, and they struck a chord with those who found the usual terminology confusing. She began running wine-tastings for her friends, and quickly found herself being asked to plan events, judge wine competitions, and even write for the newspapers. It has also pushed her to visit new places.

'People forget that wine is a product of the land,' she said. 'And it's only made in beautiful places, like the high red rocks of South Africa, or Europe's only desert in Almería, Spain. It's taken me to places that I would never have otherwise visited, even in the UK. Did you know that there's a luxury vineyard in Wales. Wales?!'

'And has it changed the actual way you travel?' I asked. 'As in, the way that you behave when you are there?'

'When I travelled somewhere previously,' she said, 'it was about me and my experience. I was *on* that place, rather than integrated with it. There was a distance. Through wine, I have come to see regions of the world as more than just a beautiful viewpoint. I learn about how they are integrated with the local culture, and, ultimately, how they affect the taste of the wine that grows there.

'Everyone in wine talks about "terroir". It's the wine's sense of place – the climate, the soil, the air – everything that makes a wine a specific product of that time, and that place. So I've become aware of what's under the surface of a region. Literally, in terms of the geology, but also in terms of the climate shaped by distant seas or mountains, and the history that led to that wine being made there.'

'And there's a human element, too?' I asked. 'The wine doesn't make itself.'

'Every wine – even in a supermarket – takes at least four or five years to make,' she said. 'And you have to tend to the vines the entire time, then harvest them and turn the grapes into the final product. That's a significant commitment. You can't make a wine without loving it, and winemakers want to share that passion.

'Before I travelled for wine, I hardly interacted with locals. Now I'm conversing with them – generally over a bottle of wine, which is a great lip-loosener – and learning about their lives and traditions. I make friends, not just acquaintances. It's deeply expanded my experience of a place. I'm tasting it, feeling it and talking to it, not just looking at it. It's so gratifying to be more intimately involved in the places that I visit.

'Travelling has also made me appreciate wine so much more because I understand the nuances and efforts that lead to the taste. I knew it conceptually through my education, but meeting the people who actually make it has enriched the experience even more. Wine has made travel more vivid, and travel has made my experience of wine more vivid.

'Actually, it's made my whole life more vivid, from my new career to the friends that I've made and the activities that I now do, such as hiking or cycling around vineyards. I'm happier than I've ever been.'

Libby's experience shows how hedonism can actually move us up Dr Fan's scale of engagement, and completely alter our experience of travel. In her case, hedonism was a springboard for learning and development, giving her a sense of purpose that actually sounds eudemonic.

Pure hedonism, however, has a shelf life.

As I spent more winters in Verbier, I stopped socialising with each new batch of seasonal workers. Most of them would be gone in a few months, so my social group shrank to those who lived there year-round. Running the chalet had its own rewards, but I found it harder to make time to improve my skiing.

Verbier was also changing around me. It had always been one of Europe's more expensive resorts, but it was going through the same tourism shift as Ibiza. The resort has incredible access to wild terrain outside the controlled boundaries, and that attracts talented skiers from around the world. Most of them earn just enough through odd-jobs to pay for accommodation and food for the season, so that they can spend as much time as possible on the slopes. But like Ibiza with its dance music, Verbier's myth – as a place that the world's best skiers flock to – became a central part of its tourism marketing.

In an echo of Ibiza's story, Verbier's businesses began to switch from the budget seasonal workers who had *created* that skiing culture to the high-earning tourists who wanted to *taste* it. Affordable accommodation was redeveloped as luxury apartments, dive bars became cocktail bars, and the hard-charging snow-hounds were replaced by people who liked the *idea* of being in a place for expert skiers. The culture changed with them.

For the Verbier veterans who had arrived in their twenties but were still there in their forties, their budgets became squeezed, and many of them left the resort. Those who clung on still skied every day and partied every night, but it felt like the resort had moved on. Their life was full of hedonism, but empty of eudaimonia, and beneath the laughter was a sadness.

That was not a life that I aspired to. Verbier had been a fantastic phase of my life and given me a sense of escapism, but it had run its course. The evenings were all blurring into one, and as I moved from ski instructing to chalet management I became less motivated to go skiing. Without that eudemonic purpose, the pure hedonistic fun felt less compelling.

One evening, I was chatting about this to a friend and her mother, who summarised it more simply than I ever could.

'Everything comes to an end,' my friend's mum said. 'Besides, there's nothing less attractive than a 30-year-old ski bum.'

I was 29. It was time to find something else.

Chapter 4

MENTORSHIP: A Moveable Feast

Someone once told me that you need three things to build a career: the skills to do the work; a portfolio to prove you can do the work; and a mentor in the industry, who can point you towards work.

After university I spent a year in Australia and New Zealand, and I began writing emails to my friends and family back home, documenting my travels with a dose of attempted humour. Some of my small audience wrote back to say that they enjoyed my reports, which inspired me to continue them during the rest of my time away. When I moved to Verbier, I turned this into a blog, with insights and advice about the resort and its surroundings.

I realised that I enjoyed telling stories about travel, and wondered if I could turn it into a career. I couldn't afford to do a master's degree in journalism, but I began attending free summer courses through Creative Skillset and the BBC. I learned how to film, edit and produce for television, and I gained some experience in scriptwriting and development.

All of this gave me some skills and a portfolio, but I still barely knew anyone in the travel industry itself. Thus began the dreaded round of networking events, and I felt like an imposter at every single one of them. The other people I met were already halfway up the storytelling ladder, with published articles or TV credits, but they generously shared their advice on pitching and press trips.

Press trips are a remarkable thing. A client (usually a tour operator, hotel or a nation's tourist board) pays travel costs for a journalist in exchange for being mentioned in a travel article. Newspapers and magazines (who the journalist pitches to) tend to be happy with this because they need travel news for their readers.

But the first press trip I was offered was not to the jungles of Costa Rica or the beaches of Italy. It was to a park in central London. And I lived in London.

Polo in the Park was a new event, held at the Hurlingham Club in Fulham. Professional polo teams competed in a three-day competition, but most attendees were just partying while the horses ran around in the background. I met Polo in the Park's marketing team at a networking session and, after I'd boldly told them that I was a travel journalist, they asked me to preview and review the event for *City AM*, a free London newspaper.

The writing was unpaid, but the thrill of seeing my name in print, next to words that I had written, was incredible. I had become a published journalist.

Public relations companies began contacting me, and sent me on trips that would get their clients' names in the paper: in Cambodia, I saw ancient cities that had been discovered using a new type of radar; in Barcelona, I visited portside bars and regional vineyards to taste sparkling wine. The trips were sensational. They gave me privileged access to places that I had only ever dreamt of visiting, and my writing improved as I wrote to the house style and deadlines of *City AM*.

One of the networking events that I attended was an adventure travel show in London. Guest speakers shared stories of their own travels, and I went to a talk by Nick Crane, a geographer, journalist and author. Ironically, for someone who presents a TV series about Britain's coast, Nick's talk was about his journey to the 'Pole of Inaccessibility': the point on the Earth's surface that is furthest from a coastline, in the desert of north-western China.

Nick had cycled there with his cousin, and he talked fondly of the people who he met along the way, and the variety of landscapes that he had to cross. The journey was so rewarding that it inspired him to pursue a career in travel storytelling.

It was dizzying to hear Nick put my own dreams into words, and empowering to know that it was possible. So, at the end of his talk, I nervously went up to speak to him and told him that I was inspired by his story. He asked me what I had done so far, and I admitted that I felt like an imposter.

'Don't do yourself down,' he said. 'You got your name in print, writing about travel, so you're a travel writer.'

Nick's reply is still one of the most reassuring and formative things that anyone has ever said to me.

'I'm just about to catch up with a friend,' he said, 'and I think that you should meet him.'

The friend turned out to be Michael Kerr, deputy travel editor of the *Telegraph* newspaper. The paper's travel section was widely regarded as one of the best, staffed as it was by experienced writers who wrote about more than just beach holidays.

Many *Telegraph* stories combined travel with history and current affairs, a style that is usually found in travel books or magazines rather than newspapers. Nick told Michael about my work and future plans, and Michael explained how he commissioned articles from freelancers.

'A large part of travel journalism,' he said, 'is informing readers about their favourite destinations: what's new, or what's interesting. But there's always a place for travel journalism that simply inspires. Readers may not want to replicate the journey themselves, but they can visit those places through the writing.'

Michael and I stayed in touch, and he helped me to tailor my ideas by framing them in a way that appealed to specific audiences. While Michael would eventually commission me to write a deeply personal article about India, he also helped me to develop a pitch about Paris, which another publication decided to pick up.

Michael had become an accidental mentor to me. But before I met him I had found mentors of a different sort, through reading travel books by authors like Bill Bryson, Eric Newby, Rory MacLean and Kapka Kassabova. Each of them has a different approach to writing because each of them has a different perspective on the world, and brings travel to life in vivid and varied ways.

Their books taught me about writing styles, but they also taught me about the authors themselves: what motivated them, and what steps they took to build their careers. One American author had a particularly distinctive style and a fascinating backstory, which made me completely rethink storytelling and travel.

*

Ernest Hemingway said, 'My aim is to put down on paper what I see and what I feel in the best and simplest way.' He did this through the 'iceberg theory' that he developed as a journalist – a minimalistic style that focused on the surface elements of an event, without exploring the underlying themes. He believed that good writing would reveal these themes through subtext, rather than by explicitly stating them, and I strove to emulate his style.

But Hemingway also said that, 'Happiness in intelligent people is the rarest thing I know.' He was fond of bullfighting, big game hunting, drinking and infidelity. He served as a medic in the First World War, lived all over the world, went through four marriages, and eventually took his own life. So whilst I admired Hemingway for being a paradigm-breaking writer, I did not want to become him.

All of the authors I admired had an origin myth – a series of experiences that inspired them, forced them to develop their writing style, and usually took them on a physical journey that they then wrote about. I pined for an experience like that of my own, and I found my version of it through reading Hemingway's *A Moveable Feast.*

It was one of the last books that he wrote, but it was about some of his earliest travel experiences, starting in 1920s Paris. A good exchange rate between the US dollar and French franc made Paris a cheap place for him to live, but it was also a hotbed of creativity, innovation and interesting people. Hemingway moved there with his wife and young son, and earned money by reporting for the *Toronto Star* while he worked on his novels.

The 1920s in Paris became known as *Les Années Folles* (the Crazy Years) for its explosion of fashion, music, art and literature. The Crazy Years evolved in Paris's galleries and literary salons, when the city was home to authors like F Scott Fitzgerald and James Joyce, the poet Ezra Pound, and artists like Salvador Dalí and Picasso. *A Moveable Feast* documents Hemingway's encounters with these creative geniuses, but it also includes detailed accounts of his writing process.

I decided to visit the Parisian sites that Hemingway mentions in *A Moveable Feast*, so that I could write it up as a travel story. Following in the footsteps of a literary hero is a common trope in travel writing, but when you are trying to build your career, a tried-and-tested format is helpful. It gives purpose to your journey, and an itinerary to follow, and it gives readers an easy entry point into the story.

An airline's in-flight magazine was delighted with my pitch (thanks to Michael's help) and my travel costs were supported by Eurostar. I wanted to see Paris through the eyes of a local, so a friend put me in touch with her Parisian cousin, who met me in the lobby of my hotel.

'Bienvenue à Paris!' said Charlotte Barré, giving me a peck on each cheek. 'So tell me – what can I show you of our beautiful city?'

'Well,' I said, 'I'm going to visit some of the cafés that Ernest Hemingway wrote about. But are there still any places like that today? Where Parisians spend time chatting to neighbours and strangers.'

'I know a place that covers both,' she said. 'Follow me!'

We jumped on the Paris Metro, swapping lines and going the wrong way before popping up in the sixth arrondissement on the Left Bank of the River Seine. This part of the city has long been associated with intellectualism, the arts and avant-garde culture. It is home to the brasseries *La Closerie des Lilas* and *Les Deux Magots*, which were frequented by Hemingway, but Charlotte bypassed them both to take me along Rue de Seine.

'Not those touristy places,' she said. 'I'm taking you somewhere properly Parisian.'

At the corner of Rue Jacques-Callot was a café-brasserie, *La Palette*. It had a terrace of tightly packed tables and yellow wicker chairs, shielded from the sun by cream canopies. A large queue was already waiting by the entrance, but there were plenty of empty tables, all of which had a small black card sitting on them, with 'Reservé' written on it in white.

Charlotte called out to a bespectacled man in a white shirt, and they embraced before launching into rapid Parisian French. I just about caught mention of '*artistes*, Hemingway, culture, and *journaliste*', which the bespectacled man nodded along to intently.

Davide de Jesus was the proprietor, and he shook my hand with a smile, then led us to one of the tables.

'Isn't this reserved?' I asked.

'Sort of,' said Davide. 'We keep them for our regulars – when they turn up, they know they will always have the best seats, just like they would at home. These seats are sacred, and they take time to be earned.'

I looked at the other patrons in the 'reservé' section: two dandyish men playing cards over coffee and cigarettes; a woman sipping wine and reading the newspaper while rocking her baby in a pram; four generations of a family eating lunch, and laughing at something in a magazine.

'Parisian cafés are more than food and drink,' Davide continued. 'They are the heart of a neighbourhood. This is the busiest tourist city in the world, so we must protect that spirit. In this area, we are surrounded by art schools and galleries,

75

and they all come to La Palette, whether they are students or teachers, artists or buyers. It becomes their home.

'We Parisians have a reputation for being prickly because we defend our sense of community. But once we know you, we open up. And Charlotte is a friend, so you pass the test. For today, anyway!'

'Students come here?' I asked, incredulously. My culinary expertise as a student had extended to kebabs and Tesco Value meal deals.

'Of course,' Davide replied. 'Back in the day, some of them even paid off their tabs with artwork, or gave us their painting palettes to hang on the wall. That's where the name comes from.'

Davide insisted on bringing us his lunch recommendations, which were a bottle of chilled rosé, sardines and steak tartare. Our table was just inches from that of our neighbour, who poured me a glass of his own wine before asking – in much slower French than Charlotte and Davide – why I was taking notes.

'Dalí?' he said, once I had explained my purpose. 'Oh, yes. I knew him. I made some furniture for him once.'

My jaw dropped, but this was no idle boast. Maurice Marty was a painter, sculptor and artist in his eighties, and he had been a contemporary of many artistic greats in the years after World War Two.

'I lived in Montparnasse,' he said, 'and went to college at the École des Beaux-Arts, round the corner. We all used to hang out in the bars, and we collaborated. I worked with César – his sculpture *Le Centaure* is not far from here.'

As I returned Maurice's generosity with the wine, he continued his tale.

'Serge Gainsbourg, the singer,' he said, 'what a character! I designed his apartment – all black and white. He told me, "Maurice, you can shake my hand. Talent is not infectious, so you risk nothing." Then he tried to seduce my wife, so I guess there was some risk after all.'

It was astonishing to be sitting in the Parisian sun, conversing with a man who was directly connected to the era that I had come to research. But it felt appropriate. Cafés like La Palette foster the culture of sharing that had led to Les Années Folles. The chairs are all cheek-by-jowl, so conversation is inevitable, friendships are made and movements are born.

'Proximity makes people equal,' said Davide. 'In these seats, your position melts. You wouldn't know if the person sitting next to you is a student, the French Spielberg, or the president's wife. They come with friends and know they can just be themselves. Égalité (equality). That proximity of chairs is a lubricant for promiscuous conversation, and a true exchange between neighbours. You feel you know them, and conviviality flows.'

Maurice told me other stories of Paris that I had not heard before, like the black jazz musicians who had come here in the 1920s to escape racism in the United States. Their music met French tradition and new styles of dance, which revolutionised the music scene, and in 1948 Paris hosted one of the world's first jazz festivals.

My head was fizzing with ideas (and wine) as I departed La Palette and made my way to Shakespeare and Company. It's a higgledy-piggledy bookshop, like a set from a Harry Potter film, which sits opposite Notre-Dame cathedral in the centre of the city. The original Shakespeare and Company bookshop was a few streets back, and it was there that Sylvia Beach – the shop's founder, who published James

Joyce's *Ulysses* – introduced Hemingway to the literary scene of Paris.

Shakespeare and Company has become something of a pilgrimage site for aspiring writers, and I enjoyed the irony of me – an aspiring writer – going there to write about this phenomenon. A friend of mine from university, Felicia Craddock, had taken this to the next level by moving to Paris and actually living inside the store.

'Sylvia Beach always offered shelter to struggling writers,' Felicia said. 'Her shop closed during the war, so when George Whitman founded this place in 1951, he took on the name and philosophy to preserve her spirit.'

'Who were the people that came here?' I asked.

'American Beat poets and writers came to Paris in the 1950s,' she said, 'in search of the magic that had inspired Hemingway's generation. They tumbled in, stayed for a few days, weeks, or even months, and then tumbled out again, so George called them his "Tumbleweeds".'

'And the bookshop still has that ethos. I stayed here when I first came to Paris. In return for a few hours' work, you can stay in the shop overnight. It's magical – you feel part of this literary heritage.'

This notion of a creative nexus is appealing, and artists from across the world still travel to Paris to work and study. They come in search of like-minded people, and try to osmotically absorb the spirits of their predecessors.

'The centre of Paris must be quite expensive these days,' I said. 'So where do they all live and hang out?'

'I live near Oberkampf, which is a bit further out,' Felicia said, 'but there are bars with open mic nights, and cafés like La Palette. Many expats come here to be creative, and the bars and cafés make it easy to connect. Maybe it's a bit more contrived and self-conscious than it was during Hemingway's era, but people come because of the heritage. It's inspiring.'

Rolf Potts is an American travel writer and author, who specialises in long-term travel. His debut book, *Vagabonding*, mixed practical travel advice and travel philosophy, and is so popular that it has run to 37 print editions.

When he was just 25, Rolf began writing a travel memoir about an eight-month van journey around North America. He found it difficult to build a compelling narrative of the journey, and it was never published, but Rolf believes that it was central to his development as a storyteller. He now shares his knowledge through travel-writing workshops in Paris.

'I focus on story structure,' he said, 'and keeping the reader in mind. But I think this advice actually pays off when you leave the classroom, in the trial-and-error process of writing and rewriting, as you learn from your mistakes and shortcomings. Then you rewrite again.'

Rolf uses the city itself to bring his lessons to life. By walking through the Parisian neighbourhoods that had once inspired the likes of Ernest Hemingway and James Joyce, he can call on their examples while teaching his students.

Many of the writers who lived in Paris wrote about creative ways to explore the city. Charles Baudelaire's 'flâneuring' encourages us to just wander a city and surprise ourselves, while Guy Debord's 'psychogeography' looks at how our emotions interact with the environment. Rolf tries to get his students to think and write with these mindsets.

'Paris is both walkable and aesthetically rich,' he said, 'which fosters a wandering, itinerant openness that you rarely find elsewhere. Encouraging students to "flâneur" their way through a place is even more effective when they are in the city that gave rise to the very concept of the flâneur. I want them to follow their own instincts.'

Rolf sends his students to the Musées d'Orsay and de Cluny, where the art – and the experience of observing it – can inspire more imaginative writing. He also encourages them to find inspiration in everyday life by visiting bars and brasseries, which is a technique that Hemingway used during his time in Paris.

Creativity can be hard to conjure up, but techniques like this give it the best possible chance of occurring. The very act of travel is creative – it displaces us, takes us away from our familiar places and routines, and gives us a new perspective on what we consider 'normal'. That's powerful when we engage in creative acts, like writing.

'Travel enables what Zen philosophers call "beginner's mind"', Rolf said. 'An attitude of openness and eagerness, and a lack of preconceptions in the face of new experiences. In experiencing the world as a child might – with engaged, optimistic, open-to-everything ignorance – your brain becomes optimised for a new kind of creativity. It is one thing to write in your home office, but something else to allow your creative mind to be caught by surprise in an unfamiliar place.'

This is what Hemingway sought when he travelled to Paris. Everything – from the language people spoke, to his access to other countries – was unfamiliar to him. It enabled that 'open-to-everything ignorance' that was hard for him to find in America. But he found something else, too, which super-charged his writing. Peers.

Hemingway and other writers regularly met at Gertrude Stein's house, to discuss their work under her critical eye. They each had their own styles and interests, but they learned from each other, encouraged each other and shared ideas and techniques from different genres. I asked Rolf if he saw his workshops in the same light as these 'literary salons.'

'In-person writing workshops create a "community of practice", Rolf said. 'Students are inspired by each other, as much as they are inspired by the teacher or teaching process. When a dozen people gather in a literary city, to dedicate themselves to writing, it creates an energy that feeds everyone.

'It also creates accountability. A chance for talented writing students to stick to deadlines, share their work and give each other feedback. That makes them better readers of their own work. Students really savour the creative energy of being around peers who are focused on the task of writing, and they try to take that focus and inspiration home with them.'

I don't actually enjoy *A Moveable Feast*. Hemingway is a cantankerous and frustrating person to spend time with. He is intolerant of others and, in his own words, he had a 'very bad, quick temper'. Conversations in the first third of the book feel unnecessarily detailed and apropos of nothing, with sentences that run on like a stream of consciousness.

Hemingway is either a snob or a purist in deriding his peers for writing to earn money, but he also wants to be successful himself, and to be well paid for his own stories. He criticises other writers' discipline and drinking behaviour, despite drinking three whiskies and two bottles of wine to prepare for a day of driving. The overwhelming impression is of smug superiority and bitterness.

And yet... Hemingway describes food so vividly that I can taste it and feel it. He conjures scenes and seasons better than a film director, and he captures people so sharply that I imagine that I can remember them from my own life. There are phrases and sentences that are achingly beautiful, and story codas that make me laugh out loud: when the poet Ralph Cheever Dunning climbs onto a roof during opium withdrawal, Hemingway tries to deliver him a bottle of the stuff, only for Dunning to chase him away with a cannonade of milk bottles. 'For a poet, he threw a very accurate milk bottle,' Hemingway says.

Hemingway believed that there was one true, perfect word for every sentence and description – the *mot juste* – and that, if you are ever stuck, you just need to write what he described as 'one true thing'. To Hemingway, it doesn't matter if your work is enjoyable to read. It just has to be true. *A Moveable Feast* is not a comedy romp or an adventure story, but an evocative immersion in a time and place. The sentence structure and vocabulary feels deceptively simple, until it strikes you with a profound insight or faithful description. Hemingway worked hard at this, saying that it often took him a whole day to write a single paragraph.

I had come to Hemingway's work because of his travels, but I stayed for the lessons in writing. When I was stuck for descriptions in my own travel writing, I would turn to Hemingway for inspiration – how did he get to the heart of a thing, and evoke its essence in a sentence? In both style and discipline, he became a mentor to me.

Hemingway's travels are often interpreted as a search for stories. But they were also a search for collaborators, teachers and a space to write. In Paris, he found people who stimulated his creativity, but they weren't all writers. He spent time with artists, composers, poets and musicians, who all taught him about breaking conventions and blending genres.

My journey to Paris gave me a paid writing commission, but it also gave me inspiration and motivation. I tried hard to capture scenes, settings and people with the depth and insight that Hemingway did, but I also realised that, to write with a similar passion and determination, I would have to write about the things that I cared about.

The search for a mentor is a powerful driver of travel, but we don't need to replicate their lives. Hemingway was a rugged white man, who loved bullfighting and hunting and wars. He was stimulated by interwar Europe and the saloons of Paris. I was a mixed-race urbanite, who had the post-Cold War hegemony and London pubs.

As much as I could emulate Hemingway's style, and learn from his life, the final lesson that he taught me was that I would have to go in search of my own interests, and discover what *I* wanted to write about.

Chapter 5

SERENDIPITY: Walking the Nile

Towards the end of my time living in Verbier, an old mate from university got in touch. Levison Wood had spent five years serving in the British Army, but had recently hung up his boots and begun a career in photography. He had seen my blog posts about travel writing and suggested that we meet up for a coffee.

'I love photography,' Lev said. 'But, like you, I really want to be a travel writer. As a lad, I read all the books by the old Victorian explorers – Burton, Livingstone, Speke and Younghusband – so expeditionary travel has always inspired me.'

Richard Burton, John Hanning Speke and David Livingstone were nineteenth-century British explorers of Africa. They mapped the lakes, rivers and ethnic groups of the Great Rift Valley, around modern Uganda, Kenya, Tanzania and Congo. Francis Younghusband travelled across the world's highest mountain ranges in the same era, surveying terrain and assessing Russian threats to British-ruled India.

All of them were members of the Royal Geographical

Society, and all of them have a complicated legacy, because their work was used in British colonial projects. But their actual expeditions were bold, because they went to places that no European had ever been to before. They were out of contact for months at a time, and depended on local guides to survive, but they also went to places that even local people avoided.

The purpose of expeditionary travel has changed since the Victorian era. The Royal Geographical Society no longer maps places for British supremacy, but instead supports research about remote communities and habitats, to help protect them from destruction.

'That's my dream,' said Lev. 'To visit places that other people overlook or avoid, and tell stories about them.

'I also want to do one big project. Not some tenuous world record – like "first person to pogo-stick to the North Pole while singing Abba" – but something that actually matters.'

Lev co-founded an expedition company, which took paying guests to countries that were misperceived as dangerous. They trekked along Afghanistan's Wakhan Corridor to track snow leopards, climbed the Zagros Mountains in Iraqi Kurdistan, and rafted the White Nile through newly independent South Sudan. The expeditions brought money to deprived and over-looked regions, and revealed local culture through the eyes of local guides.

Lev lectured about these journeys at the Royal Geographical Society, catching the attention of television production com-panies, who wanted to tell these stories to a wider audience. Lev began arranging safety and access for TV crews, and it was during one of these trips – to find the world's largest excavator, in South Sudan – that he struck upon his big idea. To walk the entire length of the River Nile.

Burton and Speke marked the source of the Nile from its outflow at Lake Victoria, but Lev wanted to start from the source of the river that flowed *into* Lake Victoria, deep in the mountains of Rwanda. The entire journey would cover 8,500 kilometres, starting in Rwanda, then following the river through Tanzania, Uganda, South Sudan, Sudan and Egypt, finishing in Alexandria, where the Nile flowed into the Mediterranean.

Lev planned to do it all in one go, and he gave himself up to 18 months to complete it. A television production company quickly jumped on board to film it, and Lev found a mate from the army to join him for the expedition. But in the middle of fundraising and planning, Lev gave me a call and asked to meet.

'Si has dropped out,' he said, meaning his mate from the army, 'so I was wondering if you fancied joining me?'

'It sounds amazing,' I said. 'But I'm doing my own stuff right now. Besides, this is your dream. I don't think I'd have the same commitment to finishing it. Perhaps you have to do it alone?'

'Maybe you're right,' he said. 'Will you come out for a few stretches though? I'll need the odd morale boost.'

Lev flew to Kigali, the capital of Rwanda, a few weeks later, then headed upstream to start his walk. I carried on in London, jealously receiving his updates, and wondering if I had made a huge mistake by saying no.

The TV company filmed key points of Lev's journey, but it was impossible to support a crew in the more remote regions. Lev was self-filming with a high-quality camcorder, but the TV company wanted someone to walk and film with him in those inaccessible sections. Lev persuaded them that I should be the one to do it, starting with a stretch of northern Uganda.

I landed at Entebbe airport at night, and Lev met me at the airport. He looked skinny but healthy, and gave me a huge hug as I walked out of passport control.

'Thank you for coming,' he said. 'This is going to be great.'

As soon as I stepped outside the airport, I was greeted with that sense of being 'elsewhere'. The heat settled on my skin and my nostrils filled with the scent of woodfires, sweat, kerosene, earth, refuse and plant blossom. We drove straight to Jinja, at the top of Lake Victoria, where Lev's guide was waiting for us.

Boston Ndoole was originally from the Democratic Republic of the Congo, but had moved to Uganda to escape civil war. He had been with Lev since Rwanda, and spoke most of the languages of the people who lived along the Nile; but Boston was far more than a translator: as a former soldier, he was a competent bushman and survivalist, as well as Lev's window into the various cultures that they encountered. He was a partner in the expedition, not just a guide.

The following morning we headed to Ripon Falls, where the Nile flows out of Lake Victoria. We were all wearing safari shirts, wide-brimmed hats and high-ankle walking boots, which Boston had tucked his trousers into. I followed suit, asking if it was to keep out ticks and spiders.

Boston laughed. 'Not at all. I just don't want the cuffs of my trousers getting dirty!'

The next morning we headed north on a track alongside the river, and Lev filled me in on the journey so far.

'Rwanda was a tough start,' he said. 'We had to go fast to stick to the schedule, but the steep terrain was tiring. The country had a strange atmosphere, because of the complex legacy of civil war and genocide. Names have been changed, so that people can't distinguish ethnic origins, and there's loads of collaborative activities, like community litter-picks.'

The river widened as we walked alongside it, and the banks gained height. Tourists from the adventure companies in Jinja were paddling rafts and kayaks down the rapids, but the buildings and settlements quickly started to peter out. Within half an hour, we were walking alone through wilderness.

'Tanzania was brutal,' Lev continued. 'We were very remote, and couldn't get much food, so Boston tried catapult-hunting birds and rodents. Then we encountered some bandits. They nicked a few bits of kit, but I'm glad it stopped at that – they had trucks and weapons.'

'I hope our little walk is less eventful,' I said.

After a few miles of walking, we arrived at our first village. There was a small store selling bottled water and fizzy drinks, and Boston began chatting to some of the local shopkeepers. A group of kids gathered around us, wondering what was going on, and Lev snapped a few photos. He showed them the results, leading to raucous bursts of laughter.

As Boston said goodbye to the shopkeepers, Lev asked him the distance to the next village.

'They say you shouldn't go there,' Boston said. 'That the people aren't friendly. But then, everyone says that about the next place. And the people at the next village will probably say the same thing about the people here. But they are more confused about the fact that you are walking, rather than taking a car.'

It was 10 a.m. and the temperature had already climbed to over 35°C. As the sweat collected behind my backpack, I was beginning to think that a car might be a good idea, but that would go against the entire spirit of the expedition. Fortunately,

Boston found a solution that would lighten our load while still allowing us to complete the entire journey on foot.

As a local guy walked past with a bicycle, Boston called him over and began explaining what we were up to. Within a few minutes we had lashed our rucksacks to the bike, and we set off as a group of four. Emmanuel the bicycle porter was now part of the team.

It was much easier to walk while only carrying a light bag, and I felt more confident about keeping up with Lev's pace. On the first day we walked 12 kilometres, so that I could acclimatise to the heat and activity, then we pushed a little further every day, until we were hitting 35 kilometres. We set off while the sun was still low, alongside kids on their way to school, who shouted '*mzungu!*' at us as we passed.

'What does that mean?' I asked Boston.

'Today it basically means "white man",' he said, 'But it's a Swahili word that translates as "the man who wanders around in circles". It dates back to the first European explorers, who did exactly that. But at least we are walking in a straight line, eh?'

There were villages every few hours, where we could stop for a drink. We took a longer break at midday, waiting for the worst of the heat to pass, and to get some food from a café or roadside stall. One day, I was tucking into a bowl of beans and rice when I asked Boston what it was called.

'Haricots viandé,' he said.

'"Meated beans"?' I asked, with my middling French.

'Yep,' Boston said, 'That's not rice. It's larvae. They let the beans rot a bit because maggots provide extra protein.'

I gingerly poked my food as Boston translated what he'd said to the watching villagers. They erupted in laughter, and I swallowed the rest of the dish along with my pride. To this day, I still don't know if he was pulling my leg.

As dusk approached we would stop at a village, where Boston would find us some accommodation, ranging from cots in a single room to an open patch of ground, to pitch our tents. Within a week we were approaching Lake Kyoga, where the Nile spread out into a shallow body of water. The distance between villages became shorter until we reached the sprawling port town of Galiraya, surrounded by rubbish dumps and piles of broken fishing nets.

Boston arranged a ride to take us across to the other side, and we clambered into a low wooden boat with an outboard motor. When Emmanuel nervously placed his bike in the prow of the boat, the gunwales barely cleared the water.

'Don't lean over the edge,' warned Boston. 'The lake's full of crocodiles. They're usually too slow to grab something passing, and prefer to ambush you at beaches, but I wouldn't take the risk.'

It took an hour to cross to the village of Namasale, which immediately felt different. The soil was redder, and the bushes less lush; but it was the people that had changed the most.

The Luo are more closely related to the people of Kenya and South Sudan than to the people of southern Uganda. The villagers in Namasale were darker-skinned, leaner and taller than anyone we had met so far, and they had a culture centred on cattle-herding and fishing, rather than farming and trading. That ethnic and economic divide means that the Luo regions of northern Uganda are more deprived than the rest of the country.

It was in Namasale that I finally understood something that had been nagging at me for a while. As we walked through

Uganda, I saw dozens, even hundreds, of young men who were struck by the same terrible affliction. It was a product of capitalism. A legacy of Western imperialism that was destroying the lives of young Ugandans.

In village after village, town after town, I saw the same tragedy. People who had once clung to the hope of a glorious future, only for it to be shattered by events beyond their control.

These poor young men... were Arsenal fans.

Now, I'm no football expert, but I would have expected Manchester City and Manchester United shirts, because of the recent and enduring successes of those teams. Back in March 2014, when we were walking the Nile, Arsenal had gone a decade without winning anything of note, yet around 60 per cent of the football shirts that I saw were in the red and white of that club.

Community pubs that showed football matches on television were named 'Highbury' or 'Emirates' (after Arsenal's stadiums), with the club's red-and-bronze crest emblazoned on their walls. I watched Arsenal play Swansea in one of these pubs, and the guy next to me reeled off stats about the linesman's prejudice against his favourite team.

My best friend, Andy Allen, has been an Arsenal fan for his entire life. He regularly cancels nights out due to heartbreak over an Arsenal defeat, and he has resigned himself to (in his words), 'a life of constant disappointment, made more painful by the false hope of a good start to the season.'

The Greek side of Andy's family settled in North London from Cyprus in the 1950s. They've been Arsenal fans for three generations, and they all have season tickets. Andy is condemned to a life of constant heartache because he is immersed in the cult of Arsenal, thanks to relatives who were raised within walking distance of the stadium. But Uganda is 6,000 kilometres from Highbury, so why were Arsenal fans in Uganda so committed to their club, despite the decade of failure? And why were they Arsenal fans in the first place?

Once we had settled into our hut in Namasale, I headed out to the village square and started asking people if I could photograph them in their football shirts. The first few were confused, but it didn't take long for word to get around.

Within minutes, dozens of men were lining up to get their picture taken. Most of them spoke English as good as mine, and one guy, Samuel – who was wearing an Arsenal shirt from the 1990s – translated for those who did not. After some initial awkwardness, conversation started to flow, and I asked them about their love of the club.

'It started in the early 2000s,' Samuel said, 'That was when we could start watching the Premier League.'

'But why Arsenal?' I asked.

'They were the best team back then,' Samuel said with a shrug. 'They went an entire season without losing, and the manager encouraged an attacking style of play, which we like. They also had lots of black players – so we could see ourselves in the team.'

'You must have only been five or six years old back then,' I said. 'Where did that enthusiasm come from?'

'Our brothers and fathers supported Arsenal, so we did too, and we are very loyal to our team. Every season we get the new shirt from Masindi market. They have counterfeit ones there before you can buy the real one in London!'

As the barriers between us slipped away, I started asking my own questions about their lives in Namasale, and Samuel showed me the lights on the lake, which fishermen used to entice prey. They fished despite the warnings from the Uganda Wildlife Authority because they wanted to feed their families, and it was hard for them to get jobs in the big cities because of prejudice against their ethnicity.

Namasale had been a dangerous place to grow up in, because of Joseph Kony and the Lord's Resistance Army. The extremist organisation had raided villages in northern Uganda, and Samuel knew of children who'd been kidnapped on their way to school, then forced to fight for Kony. In recent years the Lord's Resistance Army had been pushed out of Uganda, making it safer to move between villages, and there was a sense of hope about the future.

In just one evening, a football club in North London had built a bridge between me and the people of Namasale. We went from observing each other to engaging with each other, which made it easier to develop empathy and understanding; but I only knew anything about Arsenal because Andy always grumbled about them. Serendipity had brought Arsenal into my life, and serendipity helped me to forge relationships in this remote region of Uganda.

These sorts of interactions are accidental, but they are essential. They remind us that people in different places are fundamentally like us, with hopes and fears and dreams. They are not there for our entertainment, nor as the subject of orientalist study; they are people, whose stories matter, too.

Two months after I returned from Uganda, Arsenal won the FA Cup. Their first proper trophy in a decade. Andy was ecstatic. But I bet Namasale had a party for the ages.

It is easy to view a place only through the lens of the explorer or the visitor, and not see it through the eyes of those who live there. But in doing so we miss things that are critical to those cultures and remain ignorant of what shapes them, ranging from ethnic barriers and conflict, to the struggle for resources or the influence of a London football team.

Once you arrive somewhere and begin 'travelling', working out what to do can be difficult. Before setting out, your destination is just an idea and a map. When you arrive, it suddenly becomes a real world, with roads and restaurants and rivers and hills. How do you pass through it? How do you feel it and get to know it?

During our walk along the Nile we had a surprisingly large amount of downtime, as we sat around the campfire or waited for food at a café. I asked Lev what he found hard about his journey.

'Now that I've started it,' he said, 'I know that I will finish it. I'm pretty stubborn and dedicated when I set my mind to something, and it's just putting one foot in front of the other, really. The hardest part was getting to the start line. Dealing with all the logistics and sponsorship and TV commissions. Although that's a bit like walking, too. You just do one thing after the next, and eventually you get there.

'When it's hard, I just remind myself that it's a privilege to be on this trip. I chose to come here, and most of the people I meet don't have the resources to move beyond their local district. I'm learning a lot about myself, but I'm learning more about the places that I pass through. You can read books and watch documentaries, but that's different to seeing it for yourself.'

'But why walk it?' I asked. 'People have driven and cycled the length of Africa loads of times, so why do this on foot?'

'There's something special about walking,' Lev said. 'You arrive in a place slowly. You notice changes in the climate, or the way that villages are organised. The landscape evolves gradually, and things make sense. There's no barrier between you and the people you meet – like there is if you arrive in a car – because walking is something that everyone understands. People might think I'm mad, but they are curious about why I'm doing it, so they talk to me.'

Lev also has a mindset that made him particularly suitable for the expedition. A belief in serendipity: that you will find the people to help you out. He had found Boston when he was looking for a partner after Si dropped out. In every town or village they stopped at, he and Boston found food to eat and a place to stay. And he found new stories and history in every region he visited.

Serendipity is the belief that good and interesting things will always come along, and then overlay a sense of purpose onto them. It takes practice to develop, but travelling through the world with a sense of serendipity will alter how you view every encounter, and transform your experience of travel for the better.

I returned home shortly after Namasale, and it was another two months until I saw Lev again.

The driver of my car skidded to a halt, alongside three camels with two riders, and two men on foot. It took me a few moments to recognise my friend, who wore a white jellabiya, which is traditional among Nile Arabs, and a huge beard, which is not.

'Captain Wood, I presume?' I said. A broad smile spread across his face, and he grabbed me in a hug.

'It's good to see you,' Lev replied. 'Now, let's do some exploring!'

We were in Sudan, 150 kilometres north of the capital, Khartoum. Since our last meeting in Uganda, Lev had crossed half of South Sudan, before evacuating from the country when it erupted into civil war.

'There was nothing else I could do,' he said. 'South Sudan is an extremely dangerous place right now, and I was receiving targeted death threats. It was a difficult decision, as it means I won't walk the Nile's entire length, but to carry on would have just been reckless.'

After flying to Khartoum, Lev left the Sudanese capital on the very same day. He drove 400 kilometres to the South Sudanese border and continued his journey from there. For the next two weeks, he walked up the road that he had just driven down from Khartoum.

'Every day was the same,' he said. 'Straight road, dust and truck stops. I had all that time to reflect on having to skip part of South Sudan, and it was the closest that I came to giving up. It was made even harder because Boston couldn't get into Sudan – they wouldn't give him a visa.

'There was nothing to do during those two weeks but to think and reflect. It was very "dark night of the soul". But since I walked back into Khartoum, it's become much more interesting again. People to meet, things to see, and stuff to look forward to.'

Sudan is an unusual holiday destination. Even their embassy in London rejected my first visa application, on the grounds that 'no tourist would ever go to Sudan for three weeks'.

The embassy was mistaken. Despite the country's deep challenges and ethnic divisions, there is beauty in Sudan's landscape, and beauty in its culture and history. After an hour of walking, we crested a ridge and looked across a valley full of pyramids. Orange dunes rolled up to their bases, filling the entrances with sand. In the distance, I could see the trees that marked the banks of the Nile.

'Welcome to Meroë,' said Moez, Lev's guide in Sudan.

Meroë was the capital of the Kushite Kingdom, which invaded and ruled Egypt around 3,000 years ago. When the Kushites returned to Sudan, they brought Egyptian customs with them, including pyramid-shaped burial tombs. But while the pyramids of Egypt are now swamped by tourists and trinket-sellers, we had the Pyramids of Meroë to ourselves. There wasn't even a sign pointing to them from the highway.

'Let's camp next to them,' Moez said. 'If you wanted to do that in Egypt, you'd have to pay thousands of dollars, but this will cost us nothing. I'm trying to single-handedly improve the reputation of Sudanese tourism.'

We wandered around the empty complex, brushing away sand to reveal 2,500-year-old hieroglyphics, then pushing the sand back to protect them from erosion. Previous visitors had not been so considerate; in 1834, an Italian treasure hunter had dynamited the tops off the pyramids while searching for gold.

The two Bedouin camel-wranglers, Awad and Ahmad, settled the camels for the night, then began pranking around like Laurel and Hardy. Awad brewed sweet chai while Ahmad cooked bean stew, accompanied by bread that he somehow baked in the sand. I tried to figure out how he had done it, by building a fire in a scoop of sand, then pressing the dough into the hot ground. I just ended up with warm, sand-filled dough, which elicited fits of laughter from both of them.

As the sun edged towards the horizon, the grey and ochre landscape was stained orange and red, and the stars in the night sky were bright enough to trace the outline of the broken pyramids. The next morning, Moez woke us before dawn. Venus shone bright in the purple sky and a solitary cloud glowed orange with the first rays of the still-hidden sun. Lev wanted to start walking immediately, to cover some distance before the day got too hot, but first he handed me a white cotton shirt and trousers, which matched his own outfit.

'It's more comfortable in the heat,' he said, 'and it means we stand out less. The authorities can be a little overzealous, so it helps to avoid attention.'

The dry heat of Sudan was easier to walk in than the humidity of Uganda, and the jellabiya was much better than a safari shirt. Cars pulled over to offer us lifts, or pay for our bus tickets, and the drivers shook their heads with a smile when Moez explained the expedition.

We stopped at a café, where a group of men offered us coffee and told us about a Sufi festival near the town of Kadabas, on the other side of the river. As we rose to pay for our lunch, the waitress pointed towards a man climbing into a van and said that he had already paid for it. He looked back, smiled and waved. We hadn't even spoken to him.

Sudan's authorities were less hospitable than its citizens. Moez had been on the phone during lunch, trying to sort out approvals and permits for the next stretch of our walk. He told us that there was a problem. Halfway along the 'Great Bend' in the Nile was a dam, which was one of the most security-sensitive installations in the country. The authorities didn't want us going anywhere near it, so the only option was to go through the centre of the bend and cut straight across the Bayuda Desert. To do that we would need to be on the other side of the River Nile, on the west bank; so we would be passing the festival at Kadabas after all.

Two days, one ferry and 40 kilometres later, we were winding our way through the streets of Kadabas. Mud-walled compounds lined the roads, and donkeys chewed absent-mindedly on tufts of grass. In the distance we heard the call to prayer, and spotted a mosque and minaret on the horizon, brightly lit in green.

We turned onto a main road and into a mass of people on their way to evening prayers. They passed on a dinner invitation from the local sheikh, who had somehow heard that we were in town and apparently told everyone in Kadabas to extend the invitation on his behalf.

The sheikh was an Anglophile who had studied in Birmingham in the 1970s, and, after formally welcoming us to Kadabas, he asked Lev about his favourite villages in the Peak District. Huge plates of rice, vegetables and grilled meat were placed on the floor in front of us, and we scooped up the food with our hands and fresh bread. As evening prayers finished and tea was served, music drifted out from the courtyard in front of the mosque, and the sheikh suggested that we take a look.

Over 10,000 Sufis from across Sudan had come to Kadabas for the festival, which celebrates Muhammed's ascent to heaven. Sufism is a mystical branch of Islam that is characterised by *dhikr*,[24] an ecstatic form of worship that combines music, drumming and chanting the names of God. It was on full display in Kadabas.

A solo singer started the process, calling out words that the nearby crowd sang back to him. Drummers stood up and created ranks behind the soloist, who led his growing group

---

[24] 'Zikr' in Sudan.

in a procession around the courtyard. Dancers whirled around them as censer-bearers wafted incense into the crowd, which bowed in time to a beat that seemed to get faster with every verse. It was intoxicating, joyous and mesmerising.

Lev asked the television production team to do some research on Kadabas and the festival, but they couldn't find anything beyond a few mentions in academic papers. We were probably the first foreigners to have documented it. Had it not been for the group of men in the café, and the Sudanese government forcing us to change our route, we would not have even seen it. Serendipity had struck once again.

The temptation to absorb every sight and story of the festival was strong, but we had a desert to cross. So we left Kadabas behind and set off into the wilderness, our camels loaded with jerrycans of water and sacks of food. The sound of drumming drifted from the festival to our ears on gusts of wind, like a mischievous fairy trying to enchant us back to civilisation.

The Bayuda Desert is an ancient volcanic bulge, which pushes the River Nile eastwards, leaving a waterless, rocky landscape in its place. We had old Russian maps that suggested watering holes in the desert, but Awad and Ahmad didn't trust them. Lev decided that our best option was to get through the desert as quickly as possible, by aiming in a straight line for the town of Karima on the other side.

Every day followed the same routine: waking before dawn for a breakfast of tea, biscuits and an orange; drinking two litres of water; walking by 6 a.m. (when it was already 28°C); and stopping at 9 a.m. for a snack and more water.

By midday, it was 42°C in the shade. We would crawl into the shadow of a tarpaulin for some army rations, M&Ms and more water, then prepare for the haboob wind. This blew like a hairdryer on full power, blasting us with dust and sand and ripping the tarpaulin away from its moorings.

The temperature peaked around 2 p.m. at 49°C, and the slightest movement was exhausting. If I leaned against something, my clothing would become instantly damp with sweat – I was losing vast amounts of moisture through my skin, but I hadn't noticed it while walking because the dry air pulled it away so quickly.

By 3 p.m. the wind had usually died down to a pleasant breeze, so we would drink some more water and start to walk again. We would keep going until 7 p.m., with our pace and enthusiasm increasing as the day cooled. Dinner was another ration pack, and we were lying down to sleep by 9 p.m. On our longest day, we walked 54 kilometres.

Initially, the vast desolation of the desert was terrifying. By the third day, that terror had morphed into respect for the desert's power, and then it became something closer to affection. My daily routine had become second nature and I stopped thinking about the heat or fatigue. Anxieties that had been bubbling through my mind for months suddenly resolved, and problems seemed simple and clear. I felt almost ecstatic as I bounded through the desert.

'I know what you mean,' said Lev. 'It's the benefit of simplicity. Back home, we have to make hundreds of essentially meaningless decisions every day: pizza or sushi; tube or bus? Out here, I just go in a direction, it takes as long as it takes, and I eat the food that's available. Once I accepted that, it was liberating. I just keep walking and trust in serendipity. The noise of the unnecessary drops away, and I notice what really matters.'

On our eighth morning in the desert, we noticed palm trees on the horizon. A few hours later we were trying to thread our way through the labyrinth of irrigation ditches that lay between us and the town of Karima. It was tiring work, trudging through fine, cloying sand, and each line of palm trees hid another layer of ditches beyond it. We were considering changing direction when, all of a sudden, we broke through the final line of trees and stumbled into a field that backed onto the Nile. Lev made his way down to the water for a wash, and to remind himself of the constant thread in his journey.

An old farmer appeared, carrying tea and some fodder for the camels. He asked us to stay in his house, but we politely declined and set up camp on some flat ground. Half an hour later, as it was starting to get dark, we heard a dragging sound, and saw the farmer and his son walking out of the darkness, carrying string beds on their heads.

'If you won't sleep in my house,' said the farmer, 'then my house will come to you.'

Travel can be so bound up with daily plans and schedules that we easily lose sight of why we travel in the first place: to see new things and meet new people. Serendipity is less about travelling with a specific purpose, and more about travelling with a specific mindset: as Shakespeare's Hamlet said, 'There is nothing either good or bad, but thinking makes it so.'

When the Sudanese government forced us to change our route, Lev and I found the positives within it – we discovered a remarkable festival, and had a challenging, but sublime, journey across the desert. Serendipity comes more naturally when you don't have an itinerary to stick to, but you can bring it into any journey by seizing opportunities when they present themselves.

The master of serendipitous travel was another of Lev's

literary heroes: Patrick Leigh Fermor. While Lev took his inspiration for austere environments and expeditions from Burton and company, he took his mindset, cheerfulness and open-mindedness from Leigh Fermor.

When he was just 18, Leigh Fermor decided to walk across Europe from the Hook of Holland to Istanbul. He set off in December 1933 with just a pack of clothes and some books, intending to sleep in barns or shepherds' huts along the way. But he also created opportunities, by striking up conversations with the people he passed and offering to assist them with their work. It helped that he spoke several European languages, which endeared him to those he met, but the key to his serendipity was his willingness to share his time with people.

Leigh Fermor carried several letters of introduction to European aristocrats, who invited him to stay in their country houses. He got to know each region through the aristocrats' eyes, but by travelling on foot (as the aristocrats never would) he also saw it through the eyes of less privileged people.[25] He drank fine wine from cut-glass goblets and smoked yard-long pipes with archdukes, but he also ate roast chickens with farmers, shared bonfires with gypsies and chopped wood with foresters.

It's impossible to see any place in its entirety, but by opening himself up to serendipity Leigh Fermor saw far more of Europe than the Grand Tourists ever had. He was helped along by introductions and recommendations, but he was genuinely interested in the cultures that he encountered.

He was also an affable companion. As the historian Jan Morris said, Leigh Fermor 'makes friends wherever he goes, is as polite to tramps as he is to barons, repays all his debts, shows just the right degree of diffidence to his seniors, merriment to his peers, flirts with girls who give him duck eggs, gets drunk [and] hates hurting people's feelings.'[26]

Not all of us have the time to walk across Europe or Africa, but we can still bring serendipity into our travels. The simplest way to do so is by giving ourselves time. It's tempting to create a packed itinerary of restaurants and sights when we visit somewhere, but an empty diary is full of serendipitous potential. That allows you to reframe changes to your schedule as 'opportunities for something new,' rather than regret for what you have lost.

Time leaves space for serendipitous conversations, but it can be intimidating to know what to talk about. As a starting point, I try to read up on the history of the place that I am visiting and read novels by local authors, because everyone loves it if you know something about their culture.

You can follow also Leigh Fermor's lead, and just try to be helpful, but always keep an eye out for the unexpected or unusual. A flurry of Arsenal shirts was my window into Uganda, and it taught me more about the people of Namasale than a sit-down interview ever could.

I'm just glad that I grew up with Andy's complaints about his club.

Chapter 6

HARDSHIP: Mountains of the Mind

Back when I was working in Verbier, a friend suggested that we ski a route known as 'Stairway to Heaven'.

'It's a bit of a hike to get there,' said Sam Smoothy, 'but I promise it will be worth it.'

Sam was a professional freeride skier from New Zealand. These extreme athletes hike to the top of a mountain, ski through sections that would make a mountain goat tremble, and jump off cliffs that an eagle would avoid. But Sam had been skiing literally all his life: his mum was skiing on the day he was born. After ski-racing throughout his teens, he switched to freeride and won competitions on three continents, which made him one of the best 'big mountain' skiers in the world.

For our day in Verbier, Sam was taking it easy. After catching the ski-lifts up the mountain, we traversed a slope above one of the groomed runs, then took off our skis and attached them to our backpacks. We checked each other's avalanche transceivers and began kicking steps into the snow, using our poles for balance as we climbed towards a ridgeline.

By the time we reached the top, I was sweating despite the cold air and already felt an ache in my legs. We looked over the ridge into a wide bowl of pure snow, which was completely untouched but for a few S-shaped ski-tracks. Other than that, we were in the wild mountains. There were no barriers, no ropes, no lifts, and no one around.

I was nervous. Almost all of my skiing, including my instructor training, had taken place on groomed pistes, or on the patches of snow between them. The only time that I had skied completely untracked snow (which skiers refer to as 'powder') was back in New Zealand, with Sam. And even that was within Treble Cone ski resort, in an area that had been checked for safety by the resort team.

'You'll be fine,' Sam said. 'This is just a bit longer and deeper than Treble Cone.'

Despite his assurances, I wasn't convinced that I was up to the task. Skiing on fresh powder requires a slightly different technique to skiing on hard-packed snow, and I was worried that my lack of experience would cause me to crash. Beyond my fear of injury and embarrassment, I felt legitimately concerned about the environment itself.

The biggest danger of skiing in an area like this, outside the controlled zone of a resort, is from avalanches. Sam assessed the risk by looking at the slope's angle and aspect (how much sun it gets every day), and by studying the reports from the mountain safety teams. He also checked the snowpack for stability, by cutting into it and testing the layers of snowfall.

'The biggest mistake,' he said, 'is overconfidence. The risk of an avalanche is real, and you should always go through the checks, even if it's an area that you know well. Every snowfall, or change in temperature, alters the snowpack and alters the risk.'

Sam believed that the avalanche risk was low, but these assessments are not perfect. We had spent the previous evening practising our search and rescue skills, but if anything went wrong we would be entirely on our own. By the time a helicopter or other skiers got to us, it would be too late to help anyone buried under the snow.

The slope was shallower than the pistes that I skied every day, but my stomach was doing somersaults, and my heart was racing. The mountain seemed to bend and stretch in front of me, and all I could hear was the rush of blood in my ears. Every colour in my visual field – from the blue of the sky to the green moss on a distant rock – popped out with an intense clarity. My hands were actually shaking on the poles, and I just wanted to be off the mountain.

'I'll go first,' Sam said. 'Wait here until I finish my pitch, and I'll stop off to the side in the safe zone. Then you ski next to my line, meet me, and then we'll do the same on the next pitch.'

He tapped his poles, let his skis run straight, and then began bouncing from side to side in the snow. He turned his skis effortlessly and left a perfect track of linked half-circles in the fresh powder. As I watched him cruise down the mountain, I tried to replicate the rhythm of his bounces, feeling my boots flex in time with his movements.

After 30 textbook turns, Sam cut off to the left, and used his speed to reach the top of a small ridge. Then he stopped, turned to me and waved his pole above his head. I took a few deep breaths and pushed off.

The snow on ski-resort pistes becomes compressed during the maintenance and preparation process, so the snow pushes back against your skis as they slide across the surface. But in freshly fallen powder the snow is dry and light and fluffy; the skis go under the surface and *through* the snow. The forces build up more gradually, creating a wonderful sense of gliding weightlessness, and a Zen-like, fluid movement. It's the reason why people risk avalanches to ski on powder.

In my urgency to overcome my fear I completely forgot that powder requires a softer approach, and almost tumbled straight over the front of my skis. Then I leaned too far back and had to fight to pull my skis into the first turn, nearly losing control as I tilted to the side. By pushing both hands forward, I balanced myself over the middle of the skis, then planted a pole to make my second turn. I straightened my legs as my skis came round and fought to stay upright in the unusual forces.

By my fifth turn, I had the feel for the snow, but my body and legs were still stiff. By the tenth turn, I had the rhythm of my pole plant and leg movement, and was rocking back and forth as the friction shifted. By the fifteenth turn, I was whooping, as my skis flew through the snow like it was clouds.

The sickness in my stomach slipped away, and I felt a rush of excitement and joy. Every movement flowed together, from my toes to my fingertips, and I felt like I was connected to the snow. It was not just a physical sensation of smooth, effortless skiing, but a humming, elated energy that coursed through my mind and body: I noticed every sensation and observation in high definition; time seemed to stretch, and everything else evaporated. It was just me, my movement and the mountain.

I pulled up below Sam and looked back at my tracks. They started like zigzags, becoming more rounded as I had relaxed, until they almost matched the ones that Sam had made.

'By the look on your face,' he said, 'I'm guessing you enjoyed that.'

I didn't know what he meant. Until I realised that my cheeks hurt from grinning.

In the 1980s, a geology professor called Rainer Newberry came up with the 'Fun Scale',[27] to explain why we do hard things.

'Type 1 Fun' is classic fun, because we enjoy it as it's happening – a stroll through the countryside, dancing at a festival or enjoying beers with your mates. Type 1 Fun is familiar, easy and comfortable. You don't learn anything from it, but it's something that you would love to repeat.

'Type 2 Fun' (or 'hard fun') is unpleasant at the time, but fun in retrospect. You are at the edge of your comfort zone, and it probably hurts, so you look forward to it ending – hiking up a mountain in the rain or running a marathon. But once it's over, you are glad that you've done it. It builds fond memories, and you might even do it again because Type 2 Fun teaches us new skills and determination.

Ben Timberlake knows both types of fun well. He is the author of *High Risk,* which explores how we alter our state of mind, and he began to understand the benefits of hardship when he underwent 'Selection'[28] for 21 SAS, a Special Forces regiment of the British Army Reserve.

Selection starts with an arduous and painful segment known as 'The Hills', which mostly involves carrying a very heavy rucksack across the mountains of South Wales. You also have to navigate across them at night, in the wind and pouring rain, to reach hidden checkpoints by a certain time.

---

[28] The SAS always capitalise it, to distinguish it as a unique selection experience that is central to their identity.

Ben found it miserable, until a fellow recruit gave him a lesson in humility.

'You have to be big-headed to take the elements personally,' his friend told him. 'The mountain isn't trying to kill you, the fog isn't bad, the wind isn't in your face, the rain isn't getting you wet, and time is definitely not against you. The Hills just *are*. They don't give a fuck about who you are. Or your feelings. That's *your* baggage. You're already carrying all this kit, why carry more? Take ego out of it.'

When Ben had got through the first few marches, he felt relieved that they were over. As he got fitter, and better at navigating, he found satisfaction in the marches themselves; then, suddenly, he found that he started to enjoy them. They didn't hurt any less, but he learned to acknowledge the pain, push through it, and take his body beyond his imagined limits.

'I could show you the route of the final march on a map,' Ben told me, 'but it would barely represent the journey itself, which felt like a journey into another realm. I passed, but didn't feel particularly tough, nor like I had won. Simply that others had failed.'

'What made the difference?' I asked.

'Everyone who quit thought that Selection would be transformative, and bestow some sort of superpower on them. But the SAS badge doesn't *give* you coolness; my mates that passed *were cool to begin with*. The Regiment is cool because they were in it; not the other way round. They didn't join for public recognition or from a desire to test themselves.'

'So Selection doesn't *make* you a certain person,' I said, 'it just reveals certain qualities within people, which the SAS also wants.'

'Exactly,' he said. 'But it goes both ways: you select the Regiment, as much as the Regiment selects you. It felt like a homecoming, rather than an achievement. Selection was like the first stage on a pilgrimage – a challenge that gave me a lot of self-knowledge, but which also created a desire to wander further and to learn more.'

For Ben, the hardship of Selection was a crucible that revealed hidden qualities and capabilities. But he was not the first person to enjoy hardship in the hills. In his wonderful book, *Mountains of the Mind*, the nature writer Robert Macfarlane traces the moment that mountains went mainstream.

For much of human history, mountains were avoided. They were a supernatural domain of monsters and gods, and only visited by prophets seeking commandments. Poets and writers described mountains as places of terror, until seventeenth-century travellers began to praise them for the emotions they evoked and the natural wonders they contained.

Tourists began visiting the Alps to experience these marvels from a distance, until a confluence of new ideas drove people to enter them. Climbing the mountains to get physically higher became analogous to moral and spiritual elevation. The summit symbolised true freedom and purity, far away from the moral corruption of the cities on the plains.

'What simpler allegory of success could there be than the ascent of a mountain?' Macfarlane says in his book. 'The summit provides the visible goal, the slopes leading up to it the challenge. When we walk or climb up a mountain, we traverse not only the actual terrain of the hillside, but also the metaphysical territories of struggle and adversity.'[29]

Mountains are inherently dangerous places: there are rockfalls, avalanches and earthquakes; you can die from the cold, or run out of food; an ice overhang could collapse on you; a storm could batter you with snow and hail; and climbing gear could rip out, leaving you to tumble over a ledge.

But these very risks led to the lionisation of those who took them on. John Ruskin, the nineteenth-century philosopher, saw risk as the forge of self-development. He believed that, by seeking out danger and overcoming it, we achieved a victory that made us more 'moral'. When Darwinian natural selection was combined with concepts of self-improvement, mountain climbing became the ultimate test of manliness.

Summits can feel transcendent. From the top of a mountain, we can sweep over the plains and valleys – which we spend the rest of our lives trudging through – with a gaze. The towns and villages of civilisation – which contain all of our trials and tribulations – look distant and irrelevant. And, against the immense eternity of ice and rock, our own lives pale into insignificance.

Being in the mountains dissolves our ego and sense of self, and they subtly shift how we orient ourselves to the world. The beauty of the environment is unparalleled: light can change in a moment; weather can shift from heartbreakingly beautiful to terrifyingly brutal; and rocky peaks that were once deep beneath an ocean give us an awesome sense of deep time.

As Macfarlane says, 'They induce, I suppose, a modesty in us... and, most importantly, mountains quicken our sense of wonder... which can so insensibly be leached away by modern existence, and they urge us to apply that wonder to our own everyday lives.'[30]

Anyone can take a helicopter to the top of a mountain, but the views and emotions feel more rewarding if we have undergone a physical struggle to reach them.

'Perhaps that's the dopamine,' Ben Timberlake said when I talked to him about this.

'I thought dopamine made us repeat things,' I said.

'Exactly,' he replied. 'Each step that you take up the mountain leads to another tiny spurt of dopamine flying into your brain. That feels good, and it encourages you to repeat it and take another step, but something else happens, too. Hardship makes your brain more malleable, which makes it learn more quickly.

'Whenever you practise a new skill or behaviour, you build new connections in your brain. Dopamine burns these new pathways in, so that they are easier to go down next time. You get this "learning double-whammy": dopamine etches the new skill into your brain, and it encourages you to repeat the skill.'

'What does that have to do with risk and hardship?' I asked.

'The more intense the experience, the bigger the dopamine kick. That means the skill gets burned into your brain more firmly, so it becomes easier to do without thinking. Fighter pilots and Special Forces soldiers train in situations that simulate death because there's no bigger reward than survival. The resulting flood of dopamine supercharges their learning. The struggle is fulfilling.'

The first time we do something that's difficult or risky, we tend to panic. That makes it hard to remember the steps to follow to overcome the problem. But if we take our time to consciously get through it, the brain is rewired by dopamine and the next time we do that task, we flow more easily through the steps. Practise it enough, and the steps turn into a behaviour, then a habit, until, eventually, they become second nature.

At that point, Type 2 Fun evolves into something else.

Our dopamine system makes us learn faster when things

are harder; then it drives us to repeat the activity that gets us there. Dopamine *creates desire for the hardship itself,* not just desire for the relief at hardship's ending. But as we keep doing something hard it gets easier; we develop new skills, we get fitter, and (thanks to the dopamine) the process gradually becomes more instinctive. When that happens, we can enter a very special state of mind.

In the 1990s, a Hungarian–American psychologist named Mihaly Csikszentmihalyi published his research into happiness and fulfilment. Csikszentmihalyi interviewed people from all corners of society – ranging from farmers to surfers, and from artists to chefs – and many of them spoke about a mental state of inspired concentration that they sometimes achieved when they did certain things. The task became effortless, and they felt like they were being moved by something greater than themselves.

'The ego falls away,' Csikszentmihalyi said. 'Time flies. Every action, movement, and thought follows inevitably from the previous one. Your whole being is involved, and you're using your skills to the utmost.'[31]

Csikszentmihalyi called these moments 'flow states'.

When we face intense physical and psychological challenges, our body is flooded with hormones and neurotransmitters, creating something called the 'acute stress response', or hyperarousal. It's also known as 'fight-or-flight' because it evolved to help us deal with dangerous situations.

Adrenaline and cortisol increase our heart rate and send blood from our digestive system to our muscles. Serotonin helps our minds keep a grip on the situation, oxytocin makes us feel closer to those that we share danger with, while endo-cannabinoids keep a cap on fear. Endorphins are 100 times more powerful than morphine and help us ignore pain until the danger has passed, and dopamine makes us hyperattentive.

As with any cocktail of drugs, there are side effects. We feel cold, start shaking and get butterflies in our stomach, and time seems to slow down as our mind tries to record every detail of the event.

Once it's all over, serotonin creates a post-danger afterglow that can last for days, while endo-cannabinoids create the post-activity bliss known as 'runner's high'; endorphins mute shame and self-criticism; and dopamine's reward system burns our response into the brain.

All in all, it is a mental state unlike any other, and one that Ben is very familiar with.

'The first time you experience hyperarousal,' he said, 'it makes you stupid because adrenaline short-circuits our critical thinking. But if you are able to balance it with control, you can learn to ride it, and enter a state of extreme cool and competence, which is the "flow state". It can all feel a bit trippy and spiritual, because it creates a profound sense of connection with the people and world around us.'

Csikszentmihalyi believed that flow states require three critical components to occur: immediate and unambiguous feedback; a clear target; and a balance between our skill and the challenge in front of us. Ben had all three of these during Selection.

'The Hills gave me a clear target,' he said. 'Getting to a checkpoint by a given time. And I had feedback from my watch and my body. But it was only when my body and my mind developed with the training that my skills began to match the challenge. The flow kicked in at that sweet spot between arousal and control.'

'And the harder the task, the harder it is to reach the flow state?' I asked.

'Yes,' he said. 'But then it feels deeper when you get there. I felt free on The Hills, and I came back from each march with fewer problems than I'd started with. You need adversity – the experience has to be tough – but you have to develop competence, too. That's when the resonance kicks in. If something is hard, but you're shit at it, then you'll just suffer. Or if something's tough, but you're so competent that you find it easy, then you won't get that neurological cocktail.'

'So does it just feel nice? Or is it more than that?'

'A flow state is a moment of growth,' Ben said. 'It's a high, and it contains the insight, wisdom and clarity of a high. But because the drugs that create it are part of us, it's how we are supposed to receive them. Do it enough, and you are heading up the ladder of self-knowledge. That's why I put myself through those levels of suffering.'

Ben's journey through Selection started out as classic Type 2 Fun: awful at the time but satisfying enough to return to. Along the way, he developed the physical and mental skills to balance the challenge of The Hills, and the experience became something else: a self-actualising flow state. It involves hardship, but it is an end to pursue in itself, not just something to enjoy retrospectively.

So Type 2 Fun can evolve into a different type of fun: a flow state. But we will have to call it 'Type 4 Fun' because 'Type 3 Fun' already has a definition. And Type 3 Fun is no fun at all.

Two years after walking the Nile, Lev was on an expedition in the Himalayas, and I joined him in the Gurez Valley of Indian Kashmir. Because of its sensitive location, the valley is guarded by the Indian Army, and an officer with a massive moustache asked us to sign a waiver before we started walking.

'This terrain is rough-and-tough,' he said, 'and you have to be rough-and-tough to handle it. So, before I let you cross it, I need to know that you are fit-and-fine.'

Lev had already spent a month crossing the mountains of Afghanistan and Pakistan, while most of my training had involved fitness classes back in London. After confirming that we were, indeed, both 'rough-and-tough' and 'fit-and-fine', we headed off, with some hearty backslaps from the officer.

We were looking forward to some good old Type 2 Fun, but I had hoped that the first day would have been a bit gentler. From the valley floor, we climbed up to a 3,600-metre-high pass, where an Indian Army patrol base kept an eye on the fence between India and Pakistani-controlled Kashmir. The soldiers were so delighted to have visitors that they gave us lunch, and we descended to the next valley with full bellies.

As soon as we got to the bottom, Miraj (our guide) headed up a snow-chute. It was slippery and steep, so we had to zigzag across it to gain height, and it seemed to keep growing, no matter how much we climbed.

I was relieved when Miraj led us off the chute to a hanging meadow, which overlooked the valley we had just climbed from. We had only travelled ten kilometres that day, but we had climbed and descended 4,000 metres of altitude. Lev explained that this took the same effort as hiking for 42 kilometres over flat ground. As soon as we finished dinner, I crept into my tent and went straight to sleep.

The next morning was not any easier, as new aches and pains had sprung up overnight. The first 15 minutes of walking are always the hardest, as the body cranks slowly into action, but once it had warmed up the aches disappeared, and I was able to enjoy the views of jagged peaks dusted with snow. We camped next to a lake that night, and our third day would take us over a ridge and into the Vale of Kashmir, where we would have a week of walking on flat terrain.

There was only a headland, at the junction of two rivers, between us and our destination at Naranaag. After crossing the first river, Miraj had to drop back to help the pony-handler, Yakult, get the horses through the water.

'Just keep following the track upwards,' Miraj said, 'until you reach a shepherd's house. Then cross the pass down to Naranaag.'

Lev planned to contour around the headland, and was trying to work out the route on Google Maps. Several different tracks converged and seemed to head off in the direction we wanted, so we followed them, but they quickly narrowed to dead ends. We began retracing our steps and breaking our own trail through the bushes, but soon realised that we were lost.

We decided to head down to the river, then follow it to Naranaag. It was a horrible, slippery descent, and the path turned out to be an animal track that led to an isolated river beach, with no indication that people ever came this way. We followed the beach, but our path was blocked by crags and rockfall, which we scrambled across by clinging to plants that grew among the rubble.

We started to head upwards, to get over the rockfall, in the hope that there was another beach on the far side. I was climbing below Lev, and looking for my next handhold, when a rock whizzed off his foot, flew inches past my head and plunged into the river below. I had been climbing too close to him to react, and if the rock had hit me, it would have knocked me into the freezing water.

We only had 30 minutes of daylight left and Lev was exhausted from leading the way, but the adrenaline of the near-miss had filled me with energy and a sharp clarity about what we needed to do.

'Let's head back to the beach,' I said. 'It's flat ground, and I saw something that could be shelter. It'll be better than clinging to this cliff face in the dark, anyway.'

It was even harder going back down, and we slumped onto a patch of grass by the beach, which was actually the roof of an abandoned shepherd's hut. I gathered wood for a fire, and Lev tried to get it started. We had no food, and only a little water, but we had shelter and warmth.

We slept fitfully, and clambered out into daylight as the sound of the dawn chorus filled the gorge. We had just decided to head back up the animal track when we heard shouts from above.

Yakult had been looking for us all night, and he sang and danced in celebration when he spotted us, before handing us two rotis for breakfast. They were the best thing I had ever eaten.

We headed uphill in drizzling rain, retracing the contours onto the track we had turned off, then ascended to the treeline. The rain increased as we headed over the pass we had originally been aiming for, and we found Miraj waiting for us at the other side.

'That was the most dangerous moment of any of my expeditions so far,' Lev said.

Given everything else that he had done, that admission filled me with horror.

Type 3 Fun ('not fun') is awful at the time, and awful in retrospect. You are beyond your comfort zone, and probably in a survival situation. The whole experience is harrowing, and you would never choose to repeat it. You can't plan for it, anyway, because Type 3 Fun usually happens when Type 2 Fun goes wrong. Another phrase for it is 'a fuck-up'.

Lev and I learned something from our Type 3 escapade: the risk-fuelled, dopamine-accelerated consolidation-of-the-steps-we-took-to-survive kind; and the cognitive, slow-motion, reflection-on-what-went-wrong kind. But was that learning worth the risk? Definitely not.

Although I don't want to *repeat* the Type 3 Fun of Kashmir, it is tempting to *relive* it through storytelling. And herein lies the problem. Because, by making the mistake sound like a jolly old romp or bestowing on it some false power or prestige, I *might* encourage others to repeat it. So, just to be clear: there was no ennobling benefit from mine and Lev's little escapade. We fucked up.

Others have no compunction about glittering the turds of their mistakes.

When John Auldjo climbed Mont Blanc in 1827, he battled everything from altitude sickness to hypothermia, and only made it down thanks to his guides. This was clearly Type 3 Fun. We know it wasn't Type 2 because everything went wrong, and he never tried it again. But in his book about the climb (which sold well), Auldjo promised his audiences that the breathtaking view made the hardship worthwhile.

It's impossible to know if Auldjo actually believed this, or if he just said it to make for a better story. What we *can* say is that he helped give birth to the idea that a summit was worth risking your life for. Others followed Auldjo up Mont Blanc. Some were successful; others perished in the attempt. Both sets of stories inspired others to emulate them.

'What is both fascinating and macabre about this sequence of events,' says Robert Macfarlane in *Mountains of the Mind*, 'is how it allows us to see certain seductive, dangerous ideas – about altitude – being passed from person to person until, at last, they result in tragedy.'

'These men were attracted to the mountains by two intertwined ideas: first, the abstract notion that reaching the summit of a mountain was a worthwhile end in itself; and second, the belief that the view from a great height could be sufficiently beautiful to merit risking one's life to see it.'

During the nineteenth century, the major imperial nations (particularly Britain, France and Russia) became obsessed with reaching and naming remote places. While these expeditions were couched in scientific and geographical discovery, their core motivation was colonial: to reach a place before your rivals was to stake a claim on it. The most challenging expeditions became a matter of national pride. A sort of international sporting event, but with resources, land and indigenous people as the prize.

Polar explorers became particularly important, but the Americans and Russians focused on the North Pole, and the United Kingdom lost the race to the South Pole. So, the Royal Geographical Society turned to the so-called 'Third Pole' to win back some prestige. The world's highest mountain. Everest.

Macfarlane calls Everest, 'The greatest of all mountains of the mind. No mountain has exerted a stronger pull over more imaginations. And no one has been more attracted to Everest than George Mallory.'

Mallory tried to climb Everest three times, with an obsession that Macfarlane likens to a 'deeply selfish love affair', which 'would prove stronger than his love for his wife and family'. In June 1924, Mallory disappeared on Everest with his climbing partner Andrew Irvine while they were on their final push for the summit. His body was found 80 years later.

For Macfarlane, the changing mythos of mountains – and the ways we feel about them – seduced Mallory to his death; back in the sixteenth century, only a madman or a holy man would enter the mountains by choice, but by the time of Mallory's expeditions, 300 years of commentary had made a summit worth dying for.

Rather than acting as a salutary lesson about the price of misadventure, Mallory's own death served to deepen and disseminate the mortuary cult of mountain worship. The Royal Geographical Society called his death 'glorious', and *The Times* claimed that 'he could hardly have chosen a better end.' Mallory's wife and three children might have disagreed with that assessment.

In 1953, Edmund Hillary and Tenzing Norgay finally climbed Everest, and made it safely back down again. For the next few decades, climbing permits could only be acquired through national mountaineering associations, so Everest was the domain of professional mountaineers and their Nepalese guides, known as Sherpas. Everest saw around ten summits a year until the 1990s, when commercial operators persuaded the Nepalese government to issue more permits.

In 1996, a storm hit several expeditions as they descended from the summit, and eight people died in 24 hours. Jon Krakauer was one of the paying clients caught up in the storm, and his book about the experience, *Into Thin Air*, criticised some commercial companies for their decision-making and suggested that they were taking underqualified climbers up the mountain.

The book was a bestseller, but – in an echo of Mallory's death – it exposed a whole new audience to the idea of climbing Everest, rather than putting people off it. Ninety-eight people summited Everest in 1996; by 2019 it had reached nearly 900. The ratio of Sherpas to clients has gone from 1:5 to 2:1, as the Sherpas transitioned from aiding expert mountaineers to becoming the experts who get clients to the summit.[32]

For a while, improvements in technology, kit, logistics and weather forecasting made Everest safer, but the sheer number of people on the mountain has started to reverse that trend. As well as the dangers inherent to all mountains, Everest's height creates additional risks: above 8,000 metres is the Death Zone, where humans can only survive a short time without supplementary oxygen; and its peak sits in the jet stream, which blows at over 320 kilometres an hour.

These conditions subside for a few days every year, when everyone makes their push for the summit. Climbers have to queue for hours in the freezing cold as they wait their turn to attempt tricky sections. The biggest challenge on Everest is now traffic. The Everest-watcher Alan Arnette estimates that, of those who set out for the summit, 29 per cent succeed but around 4 per cent perish. Many of those who die are Sherpas, who build routes across dangerous sections and spend extra time on the mountain, ferrying supplies for clients who pay up to £130,000 for the privilege.[33][34]

That mixture of ambition and money can lead to terrible outcomes. A rescue in the Death Zone is incredibly difficult. Everyone up there is already exhausted, and saving someone's life requires additional resources and a large team, which can mean abandoning your own summit attempt. People have been known to walk past dying climbers and justify it by saying, 'they knew the risks. That's the deal you make if you try to climb Everest.'

Nonetheless, the appeal of Everest continues to grow. For the Sherpas, it is well-paid work in a region with few other opportunities. But the clients are there by choice.

For many of them, Everest is the pinnacle of a lifetime of mountain climbing. For others, it is the ultimate personal challenge, like an extreme version of marathon running, and some of the people who decide to summit Everest have never even climbed a mountain before. For them, Everest is not even a Mallory-like obsession but a pathway to something else: professional adventurers see it as one challenge in a bucket list; influencers exploit it for content and follows; while some consultants and life coaches even use it as a marketing tool.

'I've climbed Everest,' they say. 'Now let me tell you how to run your business.'

That reminds me of what Ben said about the recruits who failed Selection: they thought it would bestow some sort of superpower on them. But Selection does not *make* you anything. It just reveals certain traits. Perhaps mountains do this too. After all, a summit has no special powers; it just happens to be higher than any other nearby patches of rock.

'Doing hard shit,' said Ben, 'gives you increased focus, confidence and resolve to do more hard shit in life. And the more you do, the easier "more" gets. It's a virtuous circle. That's good and meaningful stuff, but you can't teach that to someone else. They have to do it for themselves.'

'There are books that promise to reveal "The Secrets of the Navy Seals" or "The Wisdom of the Kung-Fu Mountain", but these are just money-making schemes targeting the lazy and naïve. Anyone trying to sell you a shortcut is robbing you of the very adversity that makes the lesson so powerful.'

'So it's the journey that actually matters,' I said. 'The pilgrimage to reveal your character.'

'Maybe,' Ben said. 'Being a pilgrim requires wandering until you see your own life afresh. It creates micro-epiphanies, which are the mark of personal growth. Some people on Everest must be doing that. But the motivation makes the difference.'

'In what way?'

'Climbing a mountain – or doing anything hard – won't make you special, it will just reveal your traits. So if you are doing it for some kind of acclaim, it will always be disappointing. But if you are doing it for yourself, that will shine through.

'Your mate Lev's expeditions are a good example. You can tell that he absolutely loves being out there, off the beaten track. He's not doing it to *be* on the telly or to help market a business. He just wants to explore the world. Ironically, that authentic enthusiasm is what makes his programmes so appealing. He's just sharing what he loves.'

'What about the opposite then?' I asked. 'Doing hard experiences to escape something you fear?'

'This is a tricky one,' Ben said. 'Being in wilderness is definitely therapeutic, and a flight-from-self can sometimes be a welcome relief. But this should only be a short-term thing. Making a career out of it is never good for the soul. Why do you think we've got all these toffs with double-barrelled surnames pulling sleds across the ice or achieving obscure world firsts? They're running away from the trauma of boarding school or seeking external validation and public acclaim. A great adventure is unlikely to create a deep and lasting sense of self-worth.

'The difference between exploration and adventure is that exploration brings back knowledge or insights that are useful to the rest of us. That means new stories about places that we already know, and stories about the people that live there. Not just a self-aggrandising story about what you went though.

'Hard shit can be important for personal development because it leads to post-traumatic growth [which we will come back to in Chapter 8] – but that's not interesting to everyone else. Either way, purpose is the key to self-actualisation.'

You don't need to do SAS Selection or climb Everest to enjoy the benefits of hardship. It just requires spending some time outside your comfort zone. As you build skills and tolerance, those experiences will start to feel easier. And if you are really lucky, you might even experience some 'flow'.

Hardship can also be the pathway to other travel motivations. For me, it became my pathway to service.

Chapter 7

SERVICE: Front Lines

To pay the rent while I was trying to build my travel journalism portfolio, I worked in sales at a land investment company in London. Unfortunately, I discovered that they were just selling farmland at an 11,000 per cent mark-up, like a scam from *The Wolf of Wall Street.*

I quit (the director was later charged with fraud), and spent a week wandering between the media companies of East London, trying to find a job. One of them gave me a break, and I started making videos for the charity Walking With The Wounded.

Walking With The Wounded helps veterans rebuild their lives after injury, using sponsored expeditions to raise awareness. In 2011, they had taken four injured soldiers to the North Pole with Prince Harry, and their second expedition would see five wounded soldiers summiting Everest. They needed someone to do the promotional activity for the sponsor, and my background meant that I had the right combination of skills.

I could not believe my luck. The climbing team was already at Everest Base Camp, in Nepal, and my role was to trek there with four competition winners, taking photos and making videos to support the expedition sponsor – a whisky brand.

From Kathmandu, we flew to the town of Lukla in a tiny propeller-driven aeroplane, which bounced around in updraughts every time we flew over a ridge. Landing was just as rough, with a mountain wall at one end of the runway and a cliff at the other. We were met there by our guide, Lacchu Chhetri, and then we set off on the path to Everest.

On the fifth day we reached Phortse. This tiny village of around 80 people is not on the main Everest trekking route, but it was where Lacchu lived with his family.

'Life is tough up here,' he said. 'We are above the tree-line and there are few fields for growing crops, so tourism is a lifeline. I started as a porter, carrying bags, then I began running the high mountain camp for a climbing company. Now I oversee the logistics and food for Himalayan Expeditions, and guide treks to Base Camp.

'The trekking season is short, but in those months I can earn enough to look after my family, and I can send my children to school and university. So, we are dependent on tourism, but it's a good life for us.'

I headed outside as the sun disappeared behind the mountains. Phortse sits on a plateau above a flat-bottomed valley that was carved by a gigantic glacier. Fields are broken up by huge boulders, which were carried here during the last Ice Age, then left behind as the climate warmed and the glaciers retreated.

As the light faded, a full moon rose over the landscape, lighting it like an architectural outline. Ama Dablam stood nearby, looking like an arrowhead piercing the sky, and on the furthest ridgeline were Nuptse and Lhotse, which are part of the Everest range. Beyond them was Everest itself, lit by the sun that was now far beyond the horizon. A white streamer of snow and ice trailed from its summit, ripped away by the ferocious jet-stream winds.

The trails beyond Phortse were bare of vegetation, and the walking became harder as we climbed into ever-thinner air. Everyone was looking forward to the excitement of Base Camp, but when we arrived, two days later, we were met with disappointing news. Russell Brice, the expedition leader, had called off the summit attempt.

'I'm sorry,' Russ said. 'I've been guiding here for 40 years, and it is unusually warm this season. There's an ice bulge above the Khumbu Icefall that could collapse at any moment. It's not worth the risk. The mountain will be here next year.'

The soldiers' disappointment was soothed by two crates of top-quality whisky from the sponsor. These were supposed to be for a whisky-tasting that I was due to broadcast live from Base Camp that night, but the soldiers decided to start early. It made for a very entertaining programme.

Everest Base Camp was the highest point that we would sleep at, and I woke up with a pounding headache from the altitude. The soldiers were acclimatised and didn't even have a hangover, so David 'Wisey' Wiseman – an officer from the Yorkshire Regiment – decided to give us a tour of Base Camp, which sits on the Khumbu Glacier.

Wisey took us to the base of the Khumbu Icefall, where small pillars of ice, like forests of white mushrooms, erupted from the floor of a labyrinth. The whole mass rumbled and squeaked under gravity, and Wisey pointed towards a bulge above it.

'That's why Russ called off the climb,' he said. 'Doesn't look like much, but if it goes it will sweep onto the icefall. It takes about an hour to get through its avalanche path because we use ladders to cross crevasses, and every trip is a roll of the dice.'

As we headed back to our tents, I asked Wisey how he felt about the climb being cancelled.

'We've been training for two years,' he said. 'Being selected, getting fit, dealing with our injuries, learning new skills. We climbed Mont Blanc, and Manaslu, which is 8,163 metres. All of that was incredible, and was a huge achievement in itself, even if we'd never set foot on Everest. And I've made lifelong friends – all of us on this expedition lost the career we loved through injury, and being together has helped. I'm disappointed, but it's still been an incredible journey.

'And I understand Russ's decision. He knows this mountain. If he says "no", we listen. As soldiers, we accept risk as part of the job, but we don't take risks unless we have to.'

Wisey understood the consequences of risk as well as anyone. While serving on operations in Afghanistan in 2009, he was shot in the chest. The round nicked an artery and bounced around his torso, shattering his ribs, before coming to rest in his right lung. Blood and air began filling his chest cavity, making it hard for his undamaged left lung to work.

He was dragged to safety, and a medic saved his life while the firefight continued around them, but the bullet permanently damaged the nerves that control his right arm, and it is still lodged in his lung today.

'I always wanted to be a soldier,' he said. 'I was pretty good at it, and I loved it. My injury means that I won't be able to go back to my old job, and I will probably have to leave the army, which is hard. Soldiering was my purpose and identity, but this expedition has helped me build a new definition of myself and reminded me that I can be more than an ex-soldier.'

The walk back to Lukla took half the time of the ascent because there was no need to acclimatise for altitude. As we descended, the world returned to life. Cold, dry air became warmer and carried the scent of blossom and soil. Bare rock gave way to grassy fields. Ice gave way to water. Villages became more frequent, and the paths filled with people.

In Hindu metaphysics, the Himalayas are the abode of the gods. A hostile place of power that humans should only visit on pilgrimage before returning to their cities, changed by the experience and carrying new knowledge and insight. I had only been in the Himalayas for a fortnight, but the profound power of the mountains lingered in my mind.

Life at home was unchanged. None of my TV pitches had been accepted, and my travel writing was too inconsistent to pay the bills, so I went back to the office for work, and went partying at the weekends. While I was earning enough to live on, I felt frustrated by my inability to break into the career that I wanted, and I felt a constant sense of underlying anxiety at the direction my life was going.

I felt physically fit from my time in Nepal, and the conversations with Wisey about service and purpose had resonated with me because it was a path that I had nearly taken. At the end of our time at university, many of my peers had signed up to graduate jobs or master's degrees, but I had no idea of what I wanted to do.

An online 'careers guidance questionnaire' spat out three potential futures for me: prison officer, teacher or army officer. Windsor was a garrison town, and I had gone to school with the children of soldiers, so something about the army appealed to me. After going through a selection process, I was offered a place at Sandhurst (the British Army's officer training school), but I had already fallen in love with travel, so I deferred my entrance to spend a year in Australia and New Zealand.

By the time I returned, in 2007, the wars in Iraq and Afghanistan were being widely questioned, and the psycho-logical impact on soldiers was becoming apparent. My interest in the army waned as my interest in ski resorts increased, and my place at Sandhurst expired. But I still had a longing for some sense of service, so after returning from Nepal I joined my local Army Reserve unit to test the water.

The other recruits in my intake ranged from plumbers to bankers, and artists to academics. We had to attend three hours of training at the barracks every Tuesday and, every second weekend, a coach would drive us out to a training area, where we would live in the woods for two nights of 'fieldcraft'.

The Friday evenings before these field weekends were the most difficult part of the whole process. As I passed the busy bars of Shoreditch on my way to the barracks, I would be tempted to call in sick. But, every time, I would say 'just one more', and clamber onto the coach with my comrades.

And, sure enough, as I dragged my weary limbs off the coach at the end of the weekend, I would be delighted with my choice. There was a sense of collective achievement, as we all gradually moved through the tests. The 40 recruits dropped down to 20 as some quit, but those who remained became firm friends who shared hardships and achievements. Our first job as qualified soldiers was to conduct a 62-gun salute for the Queen's birthday at the Tower of London. It felt like a suitable celebration for our efforts.

For the first time in years, I felt proud of myself. Having tested the waters of military service and found it to my liking, I passed officer selection for the second time. I finally went to Sandhurst (although only for the eight-week Army Reserve course), then headed to the Brecon Beacons in Wales to do a course in infantry tactics.

The rest of those on the course were full-time officers in the regular army. They had completed 44 weeks at Sandhurst and half of the 13-week infantry course already, while I would be joining them for just two weeks. They had spent far more time in uniform than me, and most of them were a decade younger. I fully expected to make an absolute arse out of myself.

As we got off the trucks for five days of defensive operations, one of the regulars – an impossibly handsome Rifles officer named Jamie Robertson – asked what I did for work.

'Travel journalism?!' he exclaimed. 'Why the hell are you spending your time on a grim hill in Wales?'

I mumbled something about self-discipline and service, which he seemed to think was a reasonable response.

'I bet you've seen and done some cool stuff, though,' he said. 'Everyone here has the same shit stories about being late for parade, or getting thrown out of Inferno's nightclub, so it will be great to hear something different!'

We made a deal. Jamie and the rest of the section would help me with my orders and tactics, and I'd do extra shifts digging trenches while regaling them with tales from the road. It turned into a very profitable exchange, and made sitting on a freezing hillside in horizontal rain much more palatable.

After Brecon, I took up platoon command with 7th Battalion, The Rifles, in central London. Standing in front of 30 experienced soldiers (many of whom had served in Afghanistan) as a novice straight out of training was intimidating. The key relationship was with my platoon serjeant[35], Mark Polden, who had nearly two decades of experience as a soldier.

'The soldiers don't need you to be their friend,' Mark said on my first day, 'They just need you to do a good job for them. Be consistent. Look out for their interests, help them with their own development. Shield them from shit coming down from above, and explain why we are doing something. Don't micromanage what they are doing, but give them boundaries.'

We travelled to Kenya, to do an exercise at the edge of Mount Kenya, and I also visited Myanmar and the Philippines. My final big exercise, in 2017, saw me lead the platoon to Estonia, where our regular sister battalion, 5 Rifles, were on a six-month operational tour.

'You're here because of the Russians,' said the regimental sergeant major during our familiarisation brief. 'In 2014, Russia invaded Crimea, part of Ukraine. Since then, other countries that were controlled by the Soviet Union have become worried that Russia will do the same to them.

'So, Estonia has invited its NATO allies to establish a presence here, and work alongside the Estonian Defence Forces. It's called deterrence. You lot are part of that deterrence.'

For two tiring weeks, we lived and trained in Estonia's marshes and forests, and the exercise finished with a gigantic simulated battle. Over 10,000 troops from Britain, Estonia, Denmark, Canada, France and Italy were split into attacking and defending forces, with both sides escorted by referees, who decided whether a 'kill' had been successful.

---

[35] The Rifles use the spelling 'serjeant' for historical reasons. Every other regiment uses 'sergeant'.

This wasn't done in a remote training area. Our simulated battle took place in towns and villages, with soldiers crawling through people's front gardens. Locals stood on their doorsteps with sandwiches and cups of coffee, shouting if someone strayed too close to their flower-beds.

In the closing minutes of the exercise, I led my platoon behind a school to launch an ambush on an Italian armoured column. We caught them off guard, and 'destroyed' the entire group before they could respond. A mustachioed Italian officer threw open his turret hatch and pointed at the referee.

'I call an injustice!' he declared. 'I would have shooted them all.'

'They shooted you first,' replied the referee. And the Italians were out.

The sound of whistles rang across the area, and the exercise was brought to a close. Soldiers took off their helmets and introduced themselves to their simulated foes, swapping Velcro flags and squadron badges. Locals stepped off their doorsteps, handing out sweets and shaking hands. They knew that if war ever came to Estonia it would be fought on this land, and they wanted their defenders to know the territory.

On the way back to our trucks I chatted to Major Ivo, of the Estonian Defence Forces.

'Do you really think Russia would want to invade you?' I asked.

'Maybe,' Major Ivo said. 'They've been trying to undermine us for years. Cyber-attacks. Disinformation. Causing unrest. And look what they did to Ukraine in 2014. Estonians won our freedom from Russia, like Ukraine did. And now Putin wants to have an empire again.'

'And us being here helps?'

'Of course. It shows we have friends. We are a small country. It would be hard to stop Russia all on our own. If you are here, it is easier. And Putin does not want a fight with Britain and the rest of NATO. So it makes him think again.'

As we headed back to our home in the forest, I felt a huge sense of satisfaction. My soldiering had gone from tenuous to committed. From not knowing what a 'platoon' was, to leading one in a huge NATO exercise, where our very presence was making Europe safer. I was doing something useful beyond just pursuing my own interests. I had found a sense of purpose through service.

As I put more time into the Army Reserve, I actually managed to do more in the rest of my life. It gave me the scaffolding that I fitted everything else around, and it made me appreciate my free time. Up until then, I'd not been very good at self-discipline. I'd quit jobs that were frustrating, and I'd avoided difficult paths, but as I traded weekends in nightclubs for weekends in the field I began to see that commitment had its benefits. I was not always the best, but I did the best that I could.

I learned the benefits of delayed gratification and discovered that the harder path usually takes you to a better place than the easy path. Rather than moving away from discomfort, I began to tolerate it, and then even began to seek it out: when we had to move into positions for ambushes or attacks, the best location invariably required crawling through brambles and nettles; when I realised that most discomfort was not as bad as I imagined, I became more willing to just get it done.

This had a ripple effect into other parts of my life. If articles needed to be written, or press trips organised, I would just get on and do them because it would be better than leaving it until later. I began anticipating problems (such as camera footage being lost) in advance. So, if the worst happened, it felt less unexpected, and it was easier to come up with a solution.

When the Covid pandemic arrived in Britain, and the country locked down, the army supported the NHS and crewed the Mobile Testing Units. This unprecedented step, combined with fear about the virus, led to understandable anxiety across the country. Extremist groups and conspiracy theorists began sharing wild stories about military takeovers and insidious plots.

As my unit's press officer, it was my job to let the public know what we were actually doing, by keeping in touch with the press and giving them access to our sites. I also made films about our work, and trained our soldiers in media management, in case journalists turned up at the sites unannounced. The impacts of the pandemic were real, and hospitals filled up with Covid patients, so it was rewarding to serve, in my own small way, to help reduce the fear and impact of the disease.

So what does all this have to do with travel?

As well as taking me to places as diverse as Estonia, Myanmar and Kenya, the army helped me in my day job. Not only did it develop my mindset and expose me to new ideas, but it also taught me some basic skills that were useful for expeditions.

I'm not the first one to find that combination helpful – travel authors like Rory Stewart, Eric Newby and my old friend Levison Wood all spent time as soldiers before they took up their pens – but you can travel and serve without becoming a soldier.

Médecins Sans Frontières (Doctors Without Borders) takes

volunteer doctors, nurses and other health professionals to conflict and disaster zones, to provide healthcare for people who have none. They are supported by teams of drivers, translators and logisticians, and deliver that healthcare at considerable risk to themselves.

David Nott OBE is a general and vascular surgeon working in the NHS. He also volunteers with Médecins Sans Frontières and the International Committee of the Red Cross to deliver life-saving surgery and training in conflict and disaster zones. He's been to Bosnia, Afghanistan, Gaza, Chad, Darfur, Sierra Leone, Libya, Liberia, Ivory Coast, the Democratic Republic of the Congo, Sudan, Pakistan, Syria, Haiti, Iraq and Ukraine. If he were a soldier, he would need a bigger chest for all his medals.

As a young man, David watched the film *The Killing Fields* (1984), about the power of intervention by an American journalist in Cambodia. It inspired him to intervene wherever he could, and he likens his work to scooping up a child who has trapped their fingers in a door: we feel their pain, and just want to reassure them that it will be okay by showing them love and tenderness. For David, doing this for people at the most precarious time in their lives is the greatest possible use of his skills.

In late 2015, the Assad regime of Syria and its Russian allies began to deliberately target hospitals in rebel-held areas. Ninety-five per cent of doctors and nurses had fled the fighting, while regime snipers targeted pregnant women and babies, to put pressure on the rebels. David chose to go into these rebel-held areas, despite the risks, because he knew that he could have a much bigger impact in Syria than he could back at home.

In the UK David did a few operations a day, which dozens of other surgeons in his hospital had the skills to do. But in Syria he could operate on ten patients a day, and there was no one else who could perform those procedures.

David wanted to do even more, but he had seen surgeons in other conflict zones doing more harm than good by performing operations that they were unqualified to do. So he underwent additional training when he was back in Britain, to help with cases that were previously beyond him. He also began training local surgeons in Syria, where he had built strong bonds with the doctors, surgeons and nurses that he worked with.

'It was about providing a legacy,' David says in his auto-biography, *War Doctor*. 'Not just parachuting into a war zone, saving the odd life and going home [but] leaving my temporary colleagues better equipped to deal with an ongoing situation, [which] they themselves could not walk away from.'[36]

David's first foray into war surgery was during the siege of Sarajevo in 1993. One day he was in an ambulance that was shot at, and narrowly survived. That experience taught him that he loved helping others while also living his life very close to the edge.

'I have travelled the world in search of trouble,' he says in *War Doctor*. 'It is a kind of addiction, a pull I find hard to resist. It stems partly from the desire to use my knowledge as a surgeon to help people... experiencing the worst that humanity can throw at them, and partly from the thrill of just being in those terrible places... where most people have neither been, nor want to go.'

David's service-driven travel has traits of eudemonic tourism (which we explored in Chapter 3), but he's not doing a week

141

of tenuous volunteering while on holiday; he goes to which-ever country has the greatest need for his skills, and he goes purely to serve. And, while he acknowledges that the danger can be thrilling, his willingness to risk his life to help others makes his service even more remarkable.

He also talks about the guilt of leaving people behind when he has the privilege of leaving. Some locals resented what they saw as a form of war tourism, or the intervention of a foreigner who claims to know best. That drove David's desire to teach those he met, and to advocate for more intervention and aid when he got home. By grounding his service in respect for the people he was helping, David ensured that his service was not about him.

This mix of altruism and exhilaration left David more fulfilled than ever, but it was not without its cost. He lived a spartan, lonely life and often became extremely depressed after missions. He also developed post-traumatic stress disorder (which is caused by the mind finding it hard to process what it has experienced) after a particularly horrific trip to Darfur, Sudan.

In his book, *Tribe*, the anthropologist and journalist Sebastian Junger explores community and service by looking at tribal and modern-capitalist societies. He discovered that is not necessarily the trauma of being *in* a war zone that causes long-term mental illness, but returning to a society that doesn't have a sense of community.

He discusses the testimony of some survivors of adversity – ranging from Londoners during the Blitz to combat soldiers in Afghanistan and those who lived through the height of the HIV/AIDS pandemic – who say that they sometimes miss those periods of intense survival. Junger surmises that they don't miss 'the danger or loss, but the unity that these things engender.'[37]

There are many benefits to modern society, but there are costs too, ranging from stresses at work to damage to the climate and ecosystems. But the most insidious and hidden cost of modern society is the loss of community and unity, which makes us less able to recover from traumatic events. We have moved from equitable tribes that shared food and defence, to societies that normalise selfishness; societies that punish mothers who shoplift to feed their kids, but bail out bankers who wreck the economy. That breeds resentment within society, and greater levels of unhappiness.

It's beyond any of us to overturn the inbuilt hyper-individualism of modern society, but we can play our own small part in improving it. Service makes us more fulfilled as individuals and, according to the Irish psychologist H A Lyons, it can actually be good for our own wellbeing.

'When people are actively engaged in a cause,' Lyons says, 'their lives have more purpose... with resulting improvements in their mental health.'[38]

Combining travel and service can help us find a cause and a community. David realised that by serving in less wealthy countries, he could help more people more significantly than he could back at home. But you don't have to become a doctor or travel to a war zone to find fulfilling service. You just have to find somewhere that needs you.

If you teach, your skills might be valuable in a remote Himalayan village. If you work in logistics, you could help organise shipments to disaster zones. If you are a paralegal, you could potentially provide advice in refugee camps. All of these experiences will give you the chance to serve with a team of people who are trying to do some good, and those bonds will last a lifetime.

And if you don't fancy travelling to serve, you can still serve at home and make your own contribution to society. Giving blood is the simplest altruistic thing we can do. It only costs us a few minutes, and we will never meet the people who our blood helps, but it can save the life of someone who has just given birth or been in a car accident, or who has a lifelong illness.

My own service took me to amazing places. I walked within 100 metres of wild elephants in Kenya, and crossed the Brecon Beacons with a company of soldiers by the light of a full moon. I saw more sunrises than I had seen in the rest of my adult life, and huddled beneath a tarpaulin during thunderstorms. The people who I shared these experiences with are still some of my best friends, and I had the privilege of actually doing something that made the world a bit better.

When I put on my uniform, I took a break from being a struggling travel writer – plagued by self-doubt and un-certainty – and I became a trained platoon commander, looking after 30 men and women, within a regiment that had a proud record, distinguished heritage and distinct philos-ophy. I gained a sense of identity, as well as a sense of purpose.

Service made me more content, made my travel more fulfilling, and probably made me a better person. It also intro-duced me to ideas and realities that sent me on other journeys; and they changed the course of my life.

Chapter 8

EMPATHY: Beyond The New Iron Curtain

While I was in Estonia with the army in 2017, I discovered something that surprised me: around 20 per cent of Estonia's population spoke Russian as their first language. This had posed a challenge to national integration since the end of the Soviet Union, but recent actions by the Russian president, Vladimir Putin, had turned it into a question of national security.

When Russia invaded Ukraine in 2014, Putin claimed that he did so to protect Russian-speakers, and to reclaim lands that 'belonged' to Russia. That would be like the United States invading Quebec to protect English-speaking Canadians, or the British occupying Dublin because it had once 'belonged' to the British Empire.

Other countries that had once been occupied by the Russian Empire – and which had Russian-speaking populations as a result – became worried. Would Putin use the same excuse to invade *them?*

Putin offered no evidence that Russian-speakers were under

threat, but Russia had used social media and disinformation to stir up anger in Ukraine, and it was now doing the same elsewhere. Russian troll farms amplified culture wars on topics like gun control and racism in America; Russian hackers interfered in elections and Russian money corrupted referendums; Russian forces supported atrocities in Syria; and Russian agents murdered former spies in Britain.

The post-Cold War thaw was over, and a New Iron Curtain was falling across Europe. It started in Arctic Norway, travelled down the border with Finland, crossed the Baltic Sea to Estonia, then went round Latvia and Lithuania to the Russian exclave of Kaliningrad. East of Poland was the Russian-influenced nation of Belarus, and south of Belarus was Ukraine.

On the news, commentators and analysts talked about the potential for war. They discussed grand strategy, but only in terms of Russia or 'the West' (which meant France, Britain, Germany and America). What about the people living in the countries along the border? I didn't hear much from *them* on the news. What was it like to live in these places? What did the people there think about Russia and the West? Did Russian-speakers agree with what Putin said?

So, like any good travel journalist, I pulled out a map and began plotting an 8,500-kilometre route through these borderlands. Friends put me in touch with their contacts who lived along the way, and Facebook groups helped me to find many more. The *Telegraph* commissioned me to make a podcast about my journey, and I began a six-month expedition along the New Iron Curtain.

But to understand the people who lived in the borderlands, I would have to do more than just ask questions. I would need to put myself into their shoes and learn how they felt. I would need to empathise.

Empathy is the ability to understand the thoughts and feelings of another person, and to see the world from their perspective. It doesn't necessarily mean that we *feel* those same emotions, but we understand where the emotions come from.

The Dutch primatologist Frans de Waal believes that empathy probably evolved alongside mammalian parental care, so that mothers could respond to the needs of their infants. But it turned out to have other benefits, too.

De Waal studied chimpanzees, and noticed that younger chimps would spot an older chimpanzee suffering and then respond by helping them. The younger chimps had recognised an emotion in the older chimp, and acted in a way that helped them. This 'altruism' helps to build trust and cooperation within chimpanzee communities, and it even extends to the adoption of orphaned chimps from outside family groups.

Empathy allows complex social structures to form. If a chimp understands that another chimp has motivations and emotions of their own, it becomes possible to reconcile after a fight, build alliances, and even develop politics. It is the beginnings of persuasion, which is vital for group actions that require the 'buy-in' of others.

In humans, empathy is the glue that binds groups and nations together: we think people are like us, so we cooperate. It is vital in international relations – where leaders try to understand the motivations of allies and opponents – but we are more likely to misread a person's motivations if they come from a culture that we are unfamiliar with. In international relations, misunderstanding can lead to conflict.

If we only perceive groups and nations through the news or popular culture, we will never truly understand them. The best way to build empathy with other people, and to go beyond the stereotypes, is to travel and meet them for ourselves.

My journey along the New Iron Curtain began in March 2018, beneath the aurora borealis in the frozen far north of Norway, where it borders Russia on the Barents Sea. I travelled south through eastern Finland, looking over the fence into Russian territory that used to be Finnish, then took the train from Helsinki to St Petersburg.

I was nervous about the border crossing, which wasn't helped by a 15-minute passport check that involved the border guard making several phone calls, and repeatedly taking my passport out of the room. Eventually he let me through, and I walked out into Russia's second city.

St Petersburg was founded by Tsar Peter the Great in 1703, as Russia's 'Window to Europe'. It was the capital of the Russian Empire until 1917, when two revolutions set the stage for communism, the Soviet Union, and the city being renamed as Leningrad. In 1941, Nazi Germany besieged the city for two and a half years, killing over 2 million people, mostly through starvation. When communism fell in 1991, Leningrad became known as St Petersburg once again.

When I arrived in April, the cold air had a striking, clear quality that made distances seem vast, particularly from the bridges across the still-frozen Neva River. Most of the buildings were three or four storeys high, with the skyline only punctured by the spires of churches or the domes of cathedrals, and broad avenues led to grand vistas that framed grand neoclassical buildings.

In front of the Winter Palace, they were already rehearsing for the annual celebrations that mark the end of World War Two (or the 'Great Patriotic War', as it is known in Russia). I was talked through the plans by Yelena, a guide who had lived in America and Europe before she had moved home to St Petersburg.

'Victory Day is important,' she said, 'because it commemorates our defeat of fascism. Everyone in St Petersburg has a relative who fought or died in the siege, so we understand suffering, and we know the cost of not protecting our land.

'Stalin tried to make treaties with the Nazis to prevent war. We were betrayed, and we won't be fooled again. Russia has never chosen aggression, or invaded anyone, but we will protect ourselves.'

'But what about Ukraine?' I asked. 'Putin sent troops into Crimea and Donbas. That was an invasion.'

'Putin brought peace and stability to Russia. You have no idea what it was like here in the 1990s. People were being murdered in the streets. Burned alive in their homes. Chechens were bombing us. Putin came and stopped all that.'

'But what does that have to do with Ukraine?' I asked.

'Putin protects us, and he protected Russians in Crimea, who were resisting fascist oppression. This narrative about "invasion" comes from the West, who always want to keep Russia down. Those places in Ukraine should have still been part of Russia anyway.'

Not everyone in Russia agreed with Yelena.

'Putin is pushing all this propaganda about the Great Patriotic War,' said one student, who asked to remain anonymous. 'And making out that Ukraine is like Nazi Germany. It's not true, but what can we do about it? We have to pay our taxes, and I can't choose what the government does with my money. There's no real democracy here, and protestors get beaten up and thrown in jail. So everyone just keeps their head down.'

In Central and Eastern Europe, the legacy of World War Two is far more complex than the story told in Britain. To the British, the Soviet Union was our ally against the great evil of the Nazis, but to the nations squashed between the two totalitarian regimes, the communists were as dreaded as the fascists.

In 1939, the Soviet Union signed a treaty with Nazi Germany. Hidden within it was a secret agreement to divide Europe between them. They collaborated to invade Poland, where Soviet security forces massacred prisoners and absorbed the eastern half of the country. The Soviet Red Army then invaded Finland and captured territory that Russia still holds to this day.

In 1940, while the rest of the world was distracted by the German invasion of France, the Red Army and NKVD (the forerunner to the KGB) marched into Estonia, Latvia and Lithuania. They occupied them, installed puppet governments and absorbed all three countries into the Soviet Union. 170,000 people were murdered or deported to forced-labour camps in Siberia.

That was not the end of Baltic suffering. The following year, Nazi Germany reneged on its treaty and invaded the Soviet Union. Estonia, Latvia and Lithuania were captured within weeks, with some locals there initially greeting the Germans as liberators. The Soviet Union returned three years later, occupying the three countries until 1991, when they regained their freedom through the largely peaceful 'Singing Revolution.'

But the Soviets left a legacy. Under their rule, huge numbers of Estonians, Latvians and Lithuanians were killed by the KGB or sent to Siberia. At the same time, hundreds of thousands of Russians migrated to the Baltics for a better quality of life. They had families in the occupied countries and, when the Soviet Union collapsed, many of them chose to stay.

These Russian-speakers had the right to remain in their new homes, but they only gained full citizenship if they took a test in the local language. People who only spoke Russian never did this, and their loss of rights and prestige has driven resentment, which is amplified by Russian-language news channels.

The physical embodiment of this dispute stands in the military cemetery of Estonia's capital, Tallinn. It's a bronze statue of a Red Army soldier, holding his helmet beneath his left arm, with a rifle strapped across his back. When I visited, it was quiet. The monument was visible from across the cemetery, with wreaths laid at its base and carnations tucked into the soldier's helmet like a bouquet.

But the Bronze Soldier has not always been here. It was unveiled in the city centre in 1947, and named 'The Monument to The Liberators of Tallinn'. After regaining its freedom, Estonia reversed the decades of Russification that were forced upon it by Moscow, by giving streets Estonian names and moving Soviet statues to museums. The Bronze Soldier, as a war memorial built on war graves, was more complex.

'I am glad you are visiting this monument,' said Sasha, the Russian-speaking taxi driver who had dropped me at the cemetery. 'I came to Estonia with the Soviet Army in the 1980s, then stayed after independence. This monument reminds me of my forebears, who defeated fascism. It symbolises the right we have, as Russians, to live here.'

To many Estonians, the Bronze Soldier represented occupation rather than 'liberation', so, after a great deal of debate,

151

in 2007, it was moved from Tallinn city centre to the Soviet section of the military cemetery.

Some Russian–Estonians saw this as an attack on their identity and civil rights, and the move was met by protests, two nights of riots and a cyber-attack on Estonian government websites. Many analysts believe that Russia was behind the unrest, but in Riga, the capital of neighbouring Latvia, I met one Russian-speaker who understood the protestors' anger.

'The Latvians treat us like animals in our own country,' said Dimitri, a Russian–Latvian. 'My mother has lived here most of her life, but she cannot get a proper pension because she has to take a citizenship test in their language.'

'But it's the same in Britain,' I said. 'If you move there, you have to take a citizenship test in English.'

'It's stupid,' he said. 'This is our country. We built it. But the Latvians hate us because of Western Russophobia. We need to protect Russians and now, thanks to God, we have President Putin to do that. I've been to Crimea. And to Donbas. Retaking territory is the only way to protect our people. And I want Putin to do the same in Riga.'

'You want Putin to invade Latvia?' I asked.

'Yes. Half the people in Riga speak Russian, so it should be part of Russia. Crimea and Donbas have shown us what is possible. And I would support it on the ground, as Russian patriots have done in Ukraine.'

Dmitri was suggesting something quite astounding: that he would participate in an insurgency to help Russia invade and annex Latvia. The other two Russian–Latvians who were with us were shocked by Dmitri's statement. They both had Latvian citizenship, and reminded him that life in Putin's Russia was no bed of roses. They cherished their Russian heritage and language, but had no desire to see Latvia within Russia.

'Well I do,' Dmitri said. 'Any life under Putin is better than life as a slave of the West.'

After passing through Lithuania and the Russian exclave of Kaliningrad, I travelled through north-east Poland, then walked along the Augustów Canal into Belarus. I'd been told that Belarus was protective of its borders, but it took me five minutes to find the border guard when I crossed over from Poland. Eventually he appeared, with a gigantic hat and a friendly smile, offered me a cup of tea, and then drew me a map for the nearest bus stop.

In December 1991, the leaders of Russia, Belarus and Ukraine met at Viskuli mansion – deep in the Białowieża Forest that Belarus shares with Poland – to sign the papers that ended the Soviet Union. I wanted to see this place, which saw the supposed 'end of history', so when I arrived at the forest's ticket office, I was gutted to be told that 'the mansion was abandoned and should not be visited'.

That, of course, made it all the more appealing.

As I waited to collect my hire bike, I was approached by a man in uniform, who spoke excellent English and introduced himself as Zhakhary. He flashed his KGB identification,[39] and told me that I lacked the proper permissions to be in the forest, so I would have to leave. But as we chatted we discovered a mutual love of rugby, and he decided that he was happy to let me explore for a few hours.

'We Belarusians are very sensitive about our border zones,'

---

[39] When the Soviet Union ended, Belarus's security service retained the KGB name.

he explained. 'And this is a border zone. Normally you need a special pass to be here, or you would be detained for three days. But I will just return here at 3 p.m., and make sure that you get back on the bus to leave.'

I promised to see him later, typed 'Viskuli' into Google Maps and pedalled off into the forest.

Now, I *might* have gone off the tourist trail. I might even have gone past a no-entry sign. But I was compelled to see this inflection point of history. The tracks became overgrown and the signs became vaguer as the forest became quieter and the route more rutted, until I suddenly discovered a road that was as well maintained as the Mall in central London. The single-storey buildings nearby were suspiciously well-kept, and even the road markings were fresh.

I was pedalling along, checking my location against my phone, when I spotted the white plaster of a two-storey mansion. Was this the ruins of Viskuli? Google Maps said it was, and my heart leaped as I approached my goal. Then I spotted the shiny spiked fence, motion-sensitive cameras and machine gun next to the entrance. This was no abandoned relic. This was a fortress.

A guard emerged from a pillbox, asked me who I was, called out to his boss and detained me for two hours. I realised that the combination of video camera and audio-recorder in my bag might have aroused suspicion, so I tried to explain (through Google Translate) that I just loved Soviet history and wanted to see the place. Luckily, they didn't search me.

Eventually they called Zhakhary the KGB man, who must have reassured them that I was just a bumbling idiot. They apologised for the inconvenience and sent me on my way with an insistent 'Now, go!'.

I didn't need to be told twice, and got back to the gate just in time for the bus. Zhakhary looked relieved to see the back of me, and I later discovered that Viskuli is now Belarusian president Alexander Lukashenko's country house – a sort of Belarusian Chequers or Camp David, but with fewer cabinet rebellions.

The next morning, I was struggling to buy a bus ticket to the Belarusian capital of Minsk, when a man in the queue behind me offered to translate for me. When he told the ticket-lady where I was going, a look of alarm crossed her face, and she spoke urgently before pointing behind me. The man handed over some cash and told me to follow him outside, where he pushed me onto a bus and stuffed a ticket into my hand.

'This bus leaves for Minsk right now,' he said.

I dug into my wallet to pull out some cash, but he closed his hand over mine.

'A man in England did the same for me, once,' he said with a laugh. 'I never thought I'd be able to return the favour, but I guess this is fate!'

From Minsk, I took a train to the Ukrainian capital of Kyiv and, as we crossed the bridge over the wide Dnieper River, the city rose on a ridge above the shoreline. Golden onion-domes of Orthodox cathedrals pushed through a forested parkland and the gigantic Motherland Monument, holding a sword and shield above her head, loomed over it all.

As we pulled into the station, Ukrainian border guards came aboard to check passports. They were all young and friendly, telling me how to get to where I was staying, and offering advice on the best café for breakfast. Kyiv central station is a grand building and I stood in front of the gigantic digital departure board for several minutes, excited by the sense of possibility from the destinations that it listed.

155

In summer sunshine, I walked to Maidan Nezalezhnosti (Independence Square) in the city centre. In late 2013, rallies were held there to protest President Viktor Yanukovych's refusal (under pressure from Putin) to sign a cooperation deal with the European Union. After the protestors were tear-gassed by riot police, the protests grew, until hundreds of thousands of people occupied the square. It became known as the Euromaidan.

'It was like a festival,' said Anna Chornous, a journalist who reported on the protests. 'You could stand here with your arms out and, within a minute, you would have a sandwich in one hand and a cup of tea in the other. The protestors organised themselves and put forward proposals: they were not against Russia, but they wanted to build a future free from Russian influence.'

In February 2014, while the Euromaidan was still going on, Anna travelled to the city of Sochi, where Russia was hosting the Winter Olympics.

'I spoke to lots of Russians,' she said. 'And I could not comprehend what they believed about Euromaidan. They were wrong about everything. Then I saw Russian media outlets, reporting that everyone on Euromaidan was a fascist. That they wanted to kill Russians and eat children. It was unbelievable. That's when I began to understand the meaning of "fake news". It was a complete inversion of reality.'

As the Winter Olympics ended, so did the Euromaidan. Yanukovych's internal security forces had been using increasing amounts of violence and protestors had retaliated, leading to the death of 108 protestors and 13 police officers. On 22 February 2014 the Ukrainian parliament voted to remove Yanukovych, who fled to Russia and was replaced by an interim government. The event became known as the Revolution of Dignity.

In Crimea, pro-Russian protestors seized government buildings and, on 27 February, unmarked Russian troops took control of the peninsula. Russia annexed it a month later. In the Donetsk and Luhansk oblasts of Ukraine's eastern Donbas, armed militias took control of government buildings and declared independence. The Ukrainian armed forces moved in and Russia began secretly supporting the separatists, before sending in unmarked soldiers, tanks and artillery. When I arrived in Ukraine in 2018, the war in Donbas was already four years old.

'I always used to think of Ukraine as a very boring place,' said Anna. 'Nothing happened here. Many of us have relatives in Russia, and we thought of them as our "brother-country". Now... I don't know how we could forgive them for what they have done.'

One and a half million Ukrainians had to flee their homes and become 'internally displaced people'. Anna took me to the Podil district, where Galina Dzhikaeva was curating a live music and theatre performance by Ukrainians who had left the occupied territories. Galina was a theatre director who had fled Crimea after Russian security services had threatened her.

'People stopped speaking out,' she said, 'and it gradually became a police state – like in Soviet times. I was doing marches and protests until the FSB came to me and said, "If you sign this witness statement and denounce Ukraine, we will give you money for the theatre. If you don't, there will be trouble for you".'[40]

---

[40] The FSB is the Russian security service, which is descended from the KGB.

'Of course, the money would only come if I put on shows that they approved. So I refused, and left. Theatre in the Soviet Union took the place of the media, as a way to tell the truth, and they were trying to do the opposite. But when I came here, I realised that theatre can also be therapy. It's been a way for me to deal with my trauma, and for other displaced Ukrainians to tell their stories.'

One of those telling his story that day was 16-year-old Losha. He was only 12 when he fled the city of Luhansk, in Donbas.

'When I first came to Kyiv,' he said, 'it was difficult. People from the east have a harder edge, and we are used to being closed. But theatre has given me a community and helped me to integrate.

'It has been part of my therapy, too. War is caused by people being disconnected from each other. But in theatre you have to open yourself up, like you do in therapy. By telling my story honestly, I connect to people, which can help us to heal.'

When the Russian-backed insurgency in Donbas became a full-blown war, volunteer militias stopped the Russian advance. Thousands of people signed up for the armed forces, and many Ukrainians living overseas came home to fight.

'I was in Nepal,' said Maksym Mieshalkin. 'Hanging out in the forests, having fun. Then I heard about the first killing on Euromaidan, and I ran 40 kilometres back to Kathmandu, banging on the door of the Ukrainian embassy to get home.'

Maks signed up to fight and was trained in reconnaissance.

'Nothing compares to being in war,' he said. 'You are hunting an animal that is trying to hunt you. I'm not saying that to glorify it, but to give you an idea of what it feels like.'

Maks showed me a picture of the platoon that he had trained

with, and then gone to war with. Out of 18 soldiers, he was the only one still alive.

'Not everyone gets out,' he said, 'and even if we do, we lose a part of ourselves. I've found it hard to adjust from war-fighting to normal life. People in the cities forget how precious freedom is, or that people are dying to protect it. So I spend my time here in the mountains.'

The Carpathian Mountains of western Ukraine run along the border with Romania, past Hungary, to Slovakia and Poland. Their very name evokes mystery and legend, and I wanted to get a sense of the region. A guiding company had put me in touch with Maks, who I met in the city of Lviv before we took the train to Yaremche, at the edge of the mountains.

'Here, in the west of Ukraine,' said Maks, 'our Ukrainian identity was born. Whenever outsiders came here to enslave the locals, they fought back, just like we are fighting back today.

'I speak Russian, and I have a lot of Russian blood in my veins, lots of Russian family. But I love being Ukrainian. We want to find our own way in life, rather than be told what to do by Russia. To them, we will always be the slave, or the naughty younger brother that needs to be disciplined.

'The people in the east – who support Russia – they have a sickness. They just want to work and get their pension, and have the government look after everything. They have "Soviet Union" in the brain, and they don't understand what freedom is.

'I come to the mountains to feel that freedom.'

Maks was tall and rangy, loping up the mountains with ease, a cigarette permanently attached to his bottom lip. He had a long lock of hair on an otherwise shaved head, in the style of Ukrainian Cossacks, who believed that when they died they would be grabbed by the lock and taken to Valhalla, the heaven for warriors. As we walked through the hills, Maks regaled me with stories of ghosts, banshees and wolf-headed monsters.

'This was once a land of giants,' he said. 'Over time, they mixed with humans and disappeared, but the people who live here still have that fiery blood in their veins. So they're like Hagrid from Hogwarts, but angrier.'

We wound between pine trees, their branches dangling down like curly hair, along paths where bright blue slugs seemed to sniff the air and wisps of mist clung to cliffs. In a clearing, we found the Rocks of Dovbush, where Ukraine's Robin Hood had launched raids on Polish gentry after following the guidance of an eagle-shaped shaman. This was a land suffused with stories, where myth blended with history, and every corner carried a fable.

We had planned on climbing Hoverla, Ukraine's highest mountain, but clouds and lightning forced us to descend, and it became hard to find our bearings. We were looking for some shepherds to point us in the right direction when the clouds parted to reveal a hut, which had a sharp, spiky rune carved into the door. The exposed wood was still light, so the carving was fresh.

'It means "protection from lightning and evil",' said Maks. 'This would have been done by a Hutsul priest with shaman-istic knowledge. The Hutsul are the people of this region, who avoided Soviet repression because they were in the mountains, so they've kept a mix of nature-worship and Christian traditions.'

We descended the mountain without encountering any lightning or evil, although we did have to wade across the cold Prut River. When we reached Zaroslyak our luck ran out: all the hostels in town were fully booked, so we headed to the local bar and asked around for solutions.

'My aunt runs a boarding house a few miles down the road,' said Vasil, who was drinking with a fellow forester. 'But you can just crash at our hut. It's not much, but it's a roof for the night. And it's a proper Hutsul home because you can't see any other houses from it!'

The sun was already setting, and we didn't fancy any more walking, so we took Vasil up on his offer and followed him to a hut in the woods nearby. It was dark by the time we arrived, with the only light coming from a firepit, and, as four more foresters stepped from the shadows, axes glinting in the fire-light, I wondered if we had made a mistake.

All my fears disappeared when Vasil and his friends cracked out bottles of vodka and plates of salo (pork fat). We spent the night learning songs and toasts in each other's languages, before passing out on a bench in the hut.

We made it back to the train station the next morning, and I waved goodbye to Maks. My route took me through millions of acres of flat, golden wheat fields beneath a bright blue sky; the shape and colours of the Ukrainian flag, which flew above my destination at Kramatorsk train station. After Russian-backed separatists captured the cities of Donetsk and Luhansk, Kramatorsk became the regional capital of Ukrainian-controlled Donbas.

'I prefer to speak Russian,' said the hotel receptionist, when I greeted her in Ukrainian, 'but I want to be in Ukraine. The rebel areas are shit – I've visited – you can't even get good cigarettes!'

Kramatorsk was only 80 kilometres from the front line of the conflict, but it was full of cafés serving flat whites, bars selling craft beer, and restaurants with everything from vegan burgers to sushi.

Donbas is Ukraine's industrial heartland. A place of coal mines, slag heaps and chimney stacks. But there is beauty here, too. Sviatohirsk Orthodox Monastery, on the banks of the Donets River, dates back to the seventeenth century. A series of white-walled, turquoise-roofed Byzantine buildings are built into tree-lined cliffs above the river, and linked by covered staircases. If this were anywhere else in Europe, it would be a top tourist destination, but I had never even heard of it.

But I had heard of New York; just not New York, Ukraine. Its name was either a marketing ploy or a token of love from its founder to his wife, who was from the American original. In 2014 it became the front line, and, to get there, I had to join a United Nations excursion and pass through three checkpoints of increasing militarisation on the route from Kramatorsk.

New York sits on a ridge, overlooking a few kilometres of valley, with the insurgent-occupied city of Horlivka on the other side. From a hill on the edge of town, the mayor, Mykola Lenko, pointed out patches of disturbed earth, which marked the trenches of separatist troops.

'Half of those fighters came from this town,' he said. 'Before the war they were the down-and-outs, the unemployed, the alcoholics. They would come to my office, and I would help them with housing and work. But once the war started, they turned up with guns and demands.

'The Ukrainian armed forces pushed them out of New York in 2014 and 2015, and now they're just sat over there in a ditch, under Russian control. I hope they're happy.'

In the New York café, funded by the United Nations Development Programme, people tucked into mozzarella and sausage pizzas, and a rapper regaled me with stories about his travels across Ukraine. A woman, who was originally from the city of Donetsk, told me about her recent marriage to a soldier, who had come from western Ukraine to fight the separatists.

'To defeat this war,' Mayor Mykola said, 'we can't just win on the battlefield. This is how we win. By continuing our lives and being part of our country.'

The nearby city of Slovyansk was the first settlement to be seized by the separatists, in April 2014. Ukrainian forces re-captured it three months later, and the main fighting took place around an old psychiatric hospital on the city's outskirts.

Since 2015, the front lines had remained largely static. An agreement in Minsk required both sides to reduce their use of heavy weaponry, and the Organization for Security and Co-operation in Europe (OSCE) sent observers to check if they were obeying. One of the OSCE observers took me to a battle-ground outside Slovyansk, to show me what these weapons could do.

'Stay on the path,' said the observer. 'We haven't cleared the grass and there could still be mines. The Russians left boobytraps all over the place.'

It looked like a scene from a World War Two film. Not a single building had a roof. The walls were broken down at strange angles, and riddled with impact rounds from tank and artillery shells.

'It's like this the whole length of the front line,' the observer said. 'Entire settlements or towns destroyed. Putin says that he will make Ukraine unrecognisable if they threaten "Russians" in Donbas. The fear is that he will concoct some excuse to increase things. Then the whole of the region, or maybe even further into Ukraine, will look like this.'

It was the annexation of Crimea that had triggered all of this, and I knew that I had to go there to fully understand the story. The Ukrainian government gave me permission to travel into 'The Temporarily Occupied Ukrainian Territory of Crimea' and a Russian–Ukrainian, Artem Fietielia, came with me to translate. But, with no direct transport links, we had to walk the two kilometres of no man's land between border posts, then take a taxi to Simferopol.

Galina, the theatre director, had put me in touch with a friend there, who had stayed in Crimea to look after her mum. We met beneath a statue of Lenin in front of the train station, and she took me through the back entrance of a café before sitting at a table in the corner.

'I cannot stay for long,' she said, nervously. 'The security services sometimes follow me, and they will be following you, too. I can't take the risk of talking to foreigners. Sorry. Good luck on your trip. Be careful who you talk to or trust.'

Crimea took on an oppressive air after that encounter. That evening, back in our hostel, I went to the toilet around midnight and found a uniformed man standing in reception, looking through the details of the guests. He and the reception-ist stopped talking when I appeared. He nodded at her, and then left.

None of my other contacts in Crimea got back to me. Banks were unable to change our money and, when I asked why, the tellers told me, 'Because your country put sanctions on us, that's why. So now you can't get the money. Your problem.'

Unsure of what to do, I tried to generate some serendipity by walking. From Simferopol, Artem and I crossed to Bakhchysarai, which was the original Tatar capital of Crimea.

Bakhchysarai Old Town sits in a narrow green valley, with

towering cliffs on either side. The Khan's Palace in the centre
is surrounded by minarets and decorated with Arabic script;
old women walk the winding mountain paths with scarves on
their heads, and the air is full of the scent of spiced food and
grilled meat. It is like being transported across the Black Sea
to Turkey, or up through the grasslands of Central Asia.

Until the Russian Empire arrived in the eighteenth century,
Crimea was the home of the Crimean Tatars, an ethnic mix
of Central Asians, ancient Greeks, Caucasians and Persians.
They became part of the Mongol Empire and Islamised, before
coming under the stewardship of the Ottoman Empire. When
the Russian Army invaded in 1736, they signed a treaty with
the ruling Khan that guaranteed independence. Fifty years
later, Russia broke the treaty and annexed Crimea, expelling
Tatar leaders and beginning the colonisation of the peninsula.

Behind the Khan's Palace I found a Great Patriotic War
memorial, which was being spruced up by a team of workmen.
It was there that I met a Tatar businessman, who lived between
Istanbul and Crimea. Like the student in St Petersburg, he
asked to remain anonymous.

'They've been doing this since 2014,' he said. 'Restoring
Soviet memory, because many Russians migrated here during
the Soviet Union, and they want a return to those days.

'I was here when the takeover happened. There were six or
seven tanks outside my house, and soldiers everywhere, with
no markings on their clothes. Russian propaganda said it was
a "local uprising", but these soldiers were definitely from
Russia, not Crimea.

'They were drunk, so I kept my family inside because you
never know what a drunk soldier might do. And then we moved
to Istanbul as soon as possible. I come back here for work,

but I'm trying to wrap up my business because it's not a good place anymore. It's especially worrying for Tatars because Russians have never treated us well.'

In 1944, the entire Crimean Tatar population was exiled to Central Asia under the orders of the Soviet leader Joseph Stalin. They were replaced in their homeland by more migrants from Russia, and the story of that time lives on in Tatar memory today.

'Soldiers came to my grandmother's house with guns,' the businessman said. 'They had five minutes to pack everything, then they were put onto cattle trains with no idea where they were going. The conditions were horrible, and they travelled 5,000 kilometres with just one stop. Of my grandmother's eight daughters, only two survived, including my mother. Then they had to make a new life in Uzbekistan. Ten years later, Crimea became part of Ukraine, but we only came back when Ukraine gained independence in 1991.

'Under independent Ukraine, we had the Mejlis, which was basically our Tatar parliament, but Russia closed it when they took over Crimea in 2014. They began taking land from the Tatars who lived in the best places – just like they did after 1944 – and people started protesting about their rights.

'We knew someone whose son was a protestor. One day, he was arrested and disappeared, so she began asking around, to find out where he was. Two FSB men came to her door, and said to her, "You have another son, don't you? If you want to keep him, you will stop asking about the son who disappeared". So now the Crimean Tatars are leaving because of the Russians. Again.'

Artem and I got a lift to the coast and began walking towards Sevastopol. This was actually the route that the British Army had taken in 1854, during the Crimean War, and it was strange to pass through 'Inkerman' and 'Alma' and 'Balaclava' – places that that I knew from regimental battle honours, or as the names of pubs in army garrison towns.

Military trucks trundled along the road, and every few miles we passed a turn-off to a village. Locals had set up stalls at these junctions, selling wine and fruit to passing cars.

'You're walking,' said one of the vendors. 'Good. In a car you miss many things – such as meeting me! Since the sanctions, we only get Russians visiting Crimea, so it's nice that you're coming to see our land.'

He handed me a cup of white wine and a cup of red. The white tasted of sherry, and the red was like wild strawberries.

'Take a bottle,' said his wife. 'It'll give you the strength to walk to Sevastopol!'

'If I drink that bottle,' I said, 'I'll never make it.'

It was early evening when we reached Sevastopol. On the wall of a shop was a surreal mural of Putin, holding the DNA of the Russian people between his hands. We popped inside for a sandwich and drinks.

As Artem and I discussed which brand of beer to go for, the lady behind the counter began speaking to us in English, with a mild northern accent. She was from eastern Ukraine, but had lived in Bolton, and moved to Crimea just before the annexation. She asked where we came from, and Artem told her that he was from Odesa.

'My friend wants to move there,' she said, 'but I'm scared for him.'

'Why?' asked Artem.

'Well, we all know what the Ukrainians are doing to the Russians in Odesa.'

'I'm a Russian from Odesa,' said Artem. 'No one is doing anything to me.'

'Well,' she said, 'perhaps you have just been brainwashed by Ukrainian propaganda.'

'Have you ever wondered,' said Artem, 'if, maybe, the Russian propaganda is wrong?'

She stopped speaking to us after that, so we paid for our food and left.

Our final stop was Yalta, which had been the premier holiday resort in the entire Soviet Union. I was surprised to learn, from an information board in the centre of town, that Yalta is twinned with Margate, a seaside town in Kent, England. Stalin apparently suggested the twinning to Churchill during the 1945 Yalta Conference.

This happened at the Livadia Palace, on the edge of town, when Stalin, US president Franklin D Roosevelt and Winston Churchill met to divide Europe between Soviet and Western spheres of influence. This was 'Great Power Politics' at its best and worst: the leaders of the three most powerful empires on Earth deciding the futures of millions of people, regardless of what those people wanted.

A huge bronze sculpture of the three leaders stood in the palace grounds, with their knees rubbed to a shine from the hands of tourists posing for photographs. As I took my own photograph, a former fighter pilot who called himself a 'student of history' offered to tell me why the sculpture was so important to Russians.

'This was when the world respected Russia,' he said. 'When they listened to our decisions and made peace in the world. When we sat together as equals.'

'Shouldn't countries be allowed to decide their future for themselves?' I asked.

'We are a peaceful nation,' he said, 'but our concerns need to be respected and sometimes that means other countries need to make agreements with us. Stalin had a lot of special qualities. He was a good leader, and he made the world respect us. That's the kind of leader Russia needs.'

Stalin was a totalitarian dictator who murdered his rivals and ideological opponents. He sent the intelligentsia and their families to labour camps, committed ethnic cleansing and created artificial famines. Academics claim that he was responsible for the deaths of up to nine million of his own people. On top of that, he allied with Hitler to carve up Europe, and invaded the countries along Russia's border.

Was that the kind of leader the pilot wanted? Or did he just want someone who made Russians feel proud?

Artem and I headed back to the border that night. It was a beautiful, clear September evening, with the stars bright in the sky. The Russian border guards spent a long time asking me about the town of Taplow (where I was born) and wanted to know why I was wearing a NASA jumper. Did I work for NASA? Was I spying on Crimea?

'I got it at Primark,' I said. I had actually bought it at the Kennedy Space Center gift shop, but I thought that would just lead to more questions.

'And Taplow is famous for its beech trees,' I continued.

Suitably informed about London shopping and Home Counties arborealism, the Russian border guards let us pass. After walking back to the Ukrainian border post we took a bus to Mykolaiv, then a train back to Kyiv. As we rumbled back through the sunflower fields of southern Ukraine, I asked Artem how he felt about Russia and Ukraine after the trip.

'When you suggested this trip,' he said, 'I thought it was

crazy. But it's been amazing. I've learned so much, and it really pushed me outside my comfort zone.

'I've found it hard in Ukraine recently. President Poroshenko has a slogan: "Army, Language, Faith". You have to speak Ukrainian to apply for official work now, and some of my Russian-speaking mates can't get jobs because they don't speak both languages, like I do.

'Sometimes I even wondered if it would be better if Odesa *was* part of Russia, but, having seen Crimea, I don't want that. Nothing works there, and people were really scared. They believed crazy things, and they were all worried about what the rest of the world thinks of Russia.

'When we crossed back into Ukraine, I felt a weight lift off my shoulders. Now I realise what we mean by a "free country", but I think that Ukraine is making a mistake by pushing against the Russian language.

'If Russian-speakers are made to feel like we don't have a home, we will go looking for one, and that's doing Putin's work for him. But if we *own* the Russian language, and show that we are a better country, then Ukraine can become the "light" for Russian-speakers, against Russia's "dark side". That removes the power of language from Putin.'

When we arrived in Kyiv I went straight to see Galina, the theatre director, and handed her a pebble. Before I left, she had told me that she missed Crimea and just wanted a piece of her beloved homeland in her life. When I told her that the pebble was from the summit of Gora Ay Petri, a mountain that overlooks Yalta, she burst into tears and hugged me for a long time.

Six months after I returned home from Crimea, Ukraine was in the midst of a presidential election. Artem told me about a candidate he really liked. A Jewish guy, who spoke Russian as his first language, and was making Ukraine feel like a much more inclusive place again.

Artem's candidate won. His name was Volodymyr Zelenskyy.

My journey along the New Iron Curtain had a bigger impact on me than I had ever expected. There were a huge range of opinions along my route, bound up with identity and disputes over history and place. I did not agree with all of them, but I understood why people held them. I had developed empathy.

Empathy is another offspring of curious travel because we set out to understand people's motivations. Our direct experience cannot tell us everything about a place (because we only get the perspectives of the people who we meet), but personal encounters do give us raw insight into emotions, which can be hard to understand through remote research.

My new-found empathy did not fill me with hope, however. I was deeply worried by the fears and frustrations of Russian-speakers, but I was more worried by the way that those fears were being stoked by Vladimir Putin. Empathy allows us to understand how others think and feel, giving us a window into their hopes and fears, and a skilful (or manipulative) communicator can link those feelings to whatever they want. They can claim that a particular group is the cause of all our sorrows, or that doing a particular thing will make all of our dreams come true.

The Kremlin's claims did not match what I had seen in Ukraine, and Russia was making the Great Patriotic War feel like its present, rather than the past. Hints about reclaiming lands on Russia's western border felt like more than just bombastic rhetoric and bargaining tools. They felt like an objective.

I tried to get a documentary made about the New Iron Curtain, but the broadcasters told me that 'the Ukraine story is four years old'. No one picked it up, although the *Telegraph* podcast about the journey, *Edgelands*, topped the download charts.

The New Iron Curtain also inspired me to take a different journey. An educational one, on a master's degree in strategic communications at King's College London, which explored how beliefs and behaviours can be shifted and shaped. I chose to specialise in Russian propaganda.

Halfway through the course, in February 2022, Russia launched its full-scale invasion of Ukraine and my fears became painfully real. The streets of Podil were filled with gunshots, as Russian raiders were tracked down. Missiles killed evacuees at Kramatorsk train station, and part of Sviatohirsk Monastery burned to the ground. Maks went back to fighting on the front line. Anna began reporting on the war for the BBC. Artem became a refugee, and Vasil the forester was mobilised and sent to war.

I empathised with them. But now I felt their emotions, too.

Chapter 9

HEALING: The Face of Kali

My whole family was there, in the living room of my uncle's house. It was only when they brought in my father's casket that people started to cry. And it was only when they opened the casket that people started to wail.

I was 21 years old, and all I could think about was trying to do the funeral ritual correctly. My father was a Hindu, and the ceremony was conducted by a Hindu priest in Sanskrit, an ancient language that is the root of many others, but which is still used in Hindu religious settings – a bit like Latin for the Roman Catholic Church.

'The priest will explain it all to me in Hindi,' said my cousin, Sanjiv, 'then I will translate it into English, so that you understand what's going on, and what to do.'

That was the idea, anyway. The priest performed the chants in Sanskrit and muttered in Hindi to Sanjiv, who then explained it to me in English, and I became... confused. I had to repeat certain phrases in Sanskrit, and I felt like an

Englishman in Ibiza, loudly repeating schoolboy Spanish in a London accent: 'Doss serve-esses pour fah-voray.'

Compared to a Christian funeral, a Hindu funeral is like an immersive theatre experience. I had to complete a series of tasks, such as scattering flower petals, pouring Ganges water into the coffin, lighting a candle and touching my father's feet. Due to my utter confusion over the two-step translation, the priest just pushed me to where he wanted me to be.

Dad was a Hindu, but certainly not a typical one. He was the 'white' sheep of his family, as the only one of ten siblings to marry a white person (my mum), and he had no interest in introducing Barty and me to our Indian heritage. The only reason we had any interaction with our Indian family was because Mum regularly took us to our Uncle Pash's house in Maidenhead; I had to ask my relatives what the food was, what Diwali was and what the funny colourful statues around the house were (idols of Hindu gods).

When Dad's funeral was over, Uncle Pash sat me down. He had always been the head of the family, offering everyone advice and encouraging me to study hard and find a good career. Dad was stubborn, and had always ignored Pash's advice, despite having borrowed money from him to set up his first restaurant. Dad eventually stopped visiting Pash entirely, to avoid awkward questions about financial discipline and business management, and, after separating from my mum, moved to Manchester, where he eventually died of health complications related to alcohol abuse.

'Well done for today, son,' Uncle Pash said. 'There is still the matter of going to Haridwar.'

'Where's that?' I asked.

'Northern India,' my cousin Sanjiv explained. 'It's on the

River Ganges, where it comes out of the mountains. Whenever someone passes away, we take their ashes there to perform Tarpana.'

'And what's that?' I asked.

'It's a Hindu religious ritual,' Sanjiv continued, 'for your dad's soul to pass into the afterlife. A priest performs the ritual, but it is the duty of the deceased's son to go and do it. I did it for my dad when he passed away.'

Sanjiv and my other cousins had been raised in Indian households with two Indian parents, so they were immersed in Indian culture as they grew up. Having been raised by Mum, I felt about as Indian as I did French. But, more than that, I did not feel particularly obliged to do anything for my father.

There had been a time when I would have done anything to spend time with my dad. As a young boy, I even took up cricket because he had played cricket in India, and I hoped that we could play together. He only took me to the practice nets once.

The only time that I did spend with him was while visiting the pubs and restaurants of Windsor. As a restaurant and bar owner, Dad was a gregarious character. He would often keep the bar open for lock-ins with the regulars, which made him a well-known and well-liked member of the community.

Once, when I was 13 – when he had already lost his businesses through bankruptcy – Dad took me to a pub to play pool. At the time, it was only through the efforts of my mum that we were able to keep going. They were still managing the bars and restaurant, although they no longer owned them, and Mum had started working as a cleaner so that we could afford food, clothes and rent.

By this time, I was starting to understand what an alcoholic was. And even though I could recognise Dad's frailties, I still believed in him. At the pool game, he had decided to bet with his opponent. As he lined up the shot, I crossed my fingers and willed the ball into the pocket. He missed. And in doing so, he squandered an afternoon of my mum's income. I don't think I ever trusted or respected him again.

Tarpana is supposed to be completed within a year. But, seven years later, I had still not done it, and I got a phone call from Uncle Pash.

'Look,' he said. 'You've taken your time and done the travel and things that you wanted to do, but you must do this duty. Your father cannot rest, and we cannot rest, until you have done this.'

So I went to the crematorium, collected my dad's ashes and booked a flight to India. My sister and I wanted to do it together and, from the airport in Delhi, we drove to my cousin Pinki's house in the centre of the city.

'You will have to leave the ashes outside,' said Pinki. 'It is bad luck to bring them into the house.'

I left the urn in a satchel by the front door, and had the bizarre image of a thief stealing it during the night, then running off with his haul, only to open it and be confronted with a container of dust and bone-chips.

We woke very early the next morning and had a breakfast of yoghurt and roti, then Pinki told me to shave off my beard, and to dress myself in a long white kurta shirt. It felt like I was shedding one version of myself and stepping into a new character for the ritual.

The streets of Delhi were empty except for a few bullock carts and the campfires of families living next to the road. I had never seen the crowded, chaotic city without traffic, and it felt as if we had slipped into a parallel world for our journey to Haridwar. Dawn was one of those soft sunrises that I had only experienced in the subcontinent, where light seeps into the world through the haze, building in intensity until it surrounds you like a liquid.

The urban sprawl gave way to countryside, where green fields and rivers rushed past my window, as children jumped into irrigation canals and cows munched grass by the roadside. It felt like the India of myth, legend and film; until we got to Haridwar, where the journey ended in a mundane municipal car park.

The liquid dawn had given way to the fierce heat and dust of the day, as motorbikes and buses honked their horns and jostled for space. We made our way towards the river along an avenue lined with stalls. They sold trinkets, holiday tat and postcards, but also garlands and items of religious devotion: Haridwar is not just a place of funeral rites, and many Indians go there for holidays framed around pilgrimage.

We passed through a stand of trees and onto the banks of the River Ganges. It was wide and fast-flowing, with white breakers churning the water. On the horizon, I could make out the mountains that it had flowed from, and the water was still cold and grey from the glacial meltwater, which chilled the air above the river.

The riverbank ran straight, with ghats (or steps) leading down to the water. Flags and bunting fluttered from buildings as crowds of happy pilgrims splashed at the water's edge, and loudspeakers mixed prayers with security announcements. Bizarrely, the atmosphere and setting made me think of Henley Royal Regatta, but the ten-storey statue of Shiva reminded me that I was not at an exclusive rowing festival –

surrounded by Pimms and posh people wearing awful striped blazers – but at the entrance to one of Hinduism's holiest sites.

Chains led into the water for the bathing pilgrims to hold on to, and the river was flowing so fast that many of them struggled to stand up. A boy swam out into the middle and the current pulled him downstream, where he grabbed hold of a chain that dangled from a bridge and hauled himself back to the bank, laughing. He was watched over by sadhus – holy men with dreadlocks covered in white ash – who were smoking shishas full of ganja.

In the distance was a large clock tower, which looked conspicuously British in this very Hindu environment. It marked Har ki Pauri, where God (or *one* of Hinduism's 330 million gods, at least) was supposed to have stepped onto Earth from heaven. All around it were small shrines of candle-covered idols, and shacks with Hindi writing on them.

Pinki pointed to the writing on one of the shacks and said, 'Bhardwaj.'

I looked at it, and realised that she meant that the writing said 'Bhardwaj'. And I realised that I could not read my own name in its original language. I stared at it, trying to find a sense of familiarity or recognition, but felt nothing; because I could not read what it said, it had no more resonance or impact on me than the writing on nearby road signs. And that felt strangely disorientating.

'These are the stalls of the pandits,' said Pinki. 'The priests who conduct the rituals. Each pandit is responsible for certain families, and they show that by writing those names on the front of their stall. Any time our family comes here, that same priest will take care of any spiritual activities.'

Pinki spoke to the boy behind the counter, who ran off in

search of our pandit. He appeared from the backstreets wearing glasses, a moustache and a white long-shirt, smeared with some food that he was still rushing to eat. Pinki had already rung ahead to tell him why we were coming and, as he didn't speak English, he shook my hand and then started speaking to her in Hindi.

They immediately began ferociously haggling over the fee for his services. I'd heard about the mercantile nature of Hindu priests, but as I watched Pinki loudly bargaining, in the same way that she would with a street trader back in Delhi, it felt rather different to the contemplative experience that I had imagined, and a world away from the comforting Anglican vicars I was more familiar with back home.

It was all very dramatic, with Pinki shouting in shock at the pandit's opening gambit, her husband Rajesh shaking his head in disappointment at the pandit's demands, and looks of dismay from the priest as Pinki counter-offered with a lower amount. But they eventually settled on a price for the spiritual peace of my father, and we made our way down to the Ganges.

We sat on a small marble square that projected into the river. I sat closest to the water, with my sister on my right-hand side, and the priest sat opposite us. Pinki and Rajesh stood nearby. On the other side of a narrow channel of cold, grey water people splashed on the beach of an island, but the atmosphere on our bank was very different.

The priest was speaking in Sanskrit, saying words that I had to repeat, and which he repeatedly corrected me on. I wanted to know what was going on, so he translated into Hindi, which Pinki translated into English. And just like during the funeral, I was confused.

By combining Pinki's translation with what Uncle Pash had

told me, I managed to gather that Dad's soul was trapped in some kind of limbo. This ceremony would help it travel along the Ganges to the afterlife, where it could find peace.

There was the lighting of candles and the throwing of petals, until we got to a point where Barty and I had to hold a coconut, which Pinki had purchased from a stall next to the car park. The coconut had now been magically transformed into the temporary carriage of my father's soul as it was taken out of limbo, in preparation for its journey.

And then the priest asked for more money. Apparently, because it had taken me so long to come to do Tarpana, it was much harder for the priest to pull Dad's soul out of limbo, and he wanted to be properly compensated for the additional effort. He and Pinki began another round of ferocious haggling, until they settled on a price. (In case you were wondering, seven years of soul inertia in limbo costs an additional £20 to overcome).

The ritual continued until we arrived at the final act, where we had to pour the ashes into the river. This was the culmination of seven years of reflection and delays, and I was expecting a sense of closure, of satisfaction. That, even though my father had not been a great dad to me, I could do something for him. I wanted to take this moment in, to feel present in it, and to share it with my sister. I looked over at her as a tear ran down her cheek.

The moment was interrupted by the sound of our priest arguing with a neighbouring pandit, who was also conducting a Tarpana ritual. They were debating where, exactly, we should pour Dad's ashes into the river.

'*Jaldi, jaldi, jaldi!*' our priest shouted at me.

I knew what *that* meant, if only from watching cricket on television; it is what the Indian team shout at their bowlers when they want them to bowl faster. So while I was trying to absorb this meaningful moment, I was thinking about cricket, and being hurried by a Hindu priest.

My sister and I both placed our hands on the urn and poured Dad's ashes into the river. And that was it. The ceremony that I had spent years worrying about was suddenly over. The whole thing had taken ten minutes.

The priest spoke hurriedly to Pinki and dashed off, leaving me with no sense of closure or satisfaction. Barty and I followed Pinki and Rajesh through the streets of Haridwar, clinging tightly to each other, just as we had done when we first visited India as children, overwhelmed and scared by the noise and crush of people.

Pinki led us into a courtyard, where a cow munched on a pile of rubbish. The courtyard was surrounded by rooms, and in one of those rooms we found our priest, sitting cross-legged on the floor. His businesslike manner was gone, and he welcomed us with a smile, offered us tea and patted the cushion next to him, indicating that my sister and I should sit down.

In front of him was a long, thin scroll of parchment, bound along the top, and covered in Hindi writing. On the walls around us were dozens more scrolls like the first, bound in incongruous cloths of tartan print, curled up and squeezed next to each other like snail shells. He pointed at the open scroll in front of him and explained (through Pinki) that this was my family tree.

'Every time someone comes to Haridwar for Tarpana,' he said, 'they come here afterwards, to complete another ceremony. The one that we will do now.'

He wrote down the names of all of us who had come that day – me, my sister, Pinki and Rajesh. We wrote down some information about my father's life and work, and we signed it. And then we wrote down the latest update of the entire family tree.

We wrote down the names of Dad's siblings, their children, and their grandchildren, many of whom had been born since the last time someone had come to Haridwar for Tarpana. And then the priest showed us the records from those previous visits.

He showed us the first time that my name had appeared in the scrolls (Barty's name had not appeared because of the patriarchal nature of Hinduism, but we wrote it down this time). We saw the first time that Dad's name had appeared. We saw our grandfather's signature, from when he had come to perform Tarpana for *his* dad, and on and on, back through the generations.

The family tree in Haridwar goes back 13 generations – around 350 years. In other parts of India, the records of the Bhardwaj family go back 2,500 years. And all of a sudden, I felt connected to this long tribe of Indians who had done exactly the same thing as me. They had brought their loved ones' ashes to Haridwar, poured them in the river, and then, nervous and bemused and scared, they had come to this room and done this same ritual of writing their names down. I felt connected to them, and connected to my heritage.

'It is a good day to have done this,' said the priest, 'because there is an eclipse happening on this day.'

Astrology is very important to Hindus, and the solar eclipse would apparently be helpful for my dad's transition to the afterlife. So it was ironic that, by delaying my arrival for so long, I ended up doing a particularly good job for Dad's soul.

For many years, I resented my dad. I resented him for squandering our family's money, for not looking after my mum better, and for not being a proper father to me. But, through his death, we had both given each other something. I had done my duty as a son, and he had given me a connection to my heritage. It made me feel a little bit Indian.

When I explained my trip to Haridwar to my friends back home, they summarised it as a 'pilgrimage', but I felt a bit uncomfortable with that description. Yes, it was a challenging, long-distance journey that had spiritual overtones, and it had a specific objective that aided in psychological healing; but I chafed at the religious overtones of the word 'pilgrimage'.

So I asked my most pilgrim-y friend about his own experiences. Leon McCarron is an author and filmmaker from Northern Ireland, and he does a lot of walking. He has crossed the Arabian Desert on foot, walked 1,000 miles though Israel and Palestine, documented Shia pilgrimages in southern Iraq, and has walked four different versions of the Camino de Santiago, a network of pilgrimage routes across Europe.

'I think of pilgrimages as "journeys of meaning, towards a particular destination",' Leon said. 'It's probably the oldest form of elective travel – besides trade and conquest – but the purpose will differ from person to person, depending on their cultural background.

'Pilgrimage can be secular, but the best-known routes are related to a venerated individual or story from a religion – like the Catholic Camino de Santiago, or the Muslim Hajj to Mecca. In Jerusalem, I met Christians who had travelled from the Philippines and Ethiopia, just to walk on the same cobblestones that Jesus did.

'The outward, physical journey reflects an internal one. It demonstrates faith in the associated deity, and it helps pilgrims experience what the venerated individual went through – courage, resilience and tests of faith.'

'You don't have a particular faith, though,' I said. 'So why follow religious routes?'

'In Ireland we talk about "thin places", Leon said, 'Where the realms of heaven and earth are closer together than else-where. Even though I wasn't raised in a particular faith, I'm attracted to those places because I feel something powerful there.

'Pilgrimage paths are similar. When you walk on them, you absorb their thoughtfulness and purpose. I grew up in a country divided by different branches of Christianity, and many of the conflicts that affect the world today have their origins in a bunch of revolutionary thinkers, who wandered around the mountains and deserts of the Middle East. Walking those routes helped me to make sense of those traditions, and of the people who are animated by those stories.'

Leon also writes about the cultures that emerge around pilgrimage itself. In 2018 he joined the Arba'een, a Shia Muslim pilgrimage in southern Iraq that sees over 20 million people walking the 75 kilometres from Najaf to Karbala, in memory of an event that crystallised the Shia sect of Islam.

'Very little money exchanges hands on Arba'een,' Leon said. 'Shia Muslims donate money for pilgrim hospitality, and people who live along the route use that money to provide hospitality tents – with blankets and water and food – for the pilgrims.

'The very best attributes of humanity come to the surface in pilgrimage: hospitality, openness, vulnerability, purpose, strength, resilience, compassion. It's hard to be angry, or conceited, or selfish, or mean-spirited when you are surrounded by people doing good.'

In recent years, religious pilgrimage routes have become popular with secular pilgrims, who recognise the power of walking with purpose. The Camino de Santiago is a series of routes that meet in France, then cross the Pyrenees to join other routes from southern Spain and Portugal. They all lead to the Santiago de Compostela Cathedral in Galicia – the north-western region of Spain that sits above Portugal.

The Camino was a major pilgrimage route in the Middle Ages, but by the 1980s only a few hundred people were walking it each year. Its popularity soared in the 1990s and, in 2019, over 300,000 people walked at least some of it.

'The first time I walked it was a decade ago,' said Leon. 'Back then, I just wanted to do long-distance hikes in interesting places, which usually requires tents and logistics. But on the Camino, there's no hard borders, the infrastructure is good, and there's subsidised hostels every five or ten kilometres. I just liked the ease of it.

'Most pilgrims weren't on the Camino for religious reasons. Most were at transitory points in their lives, having left relationships or jobs, or dealing with bereavement. A pilgrimage is therapeutic because it lets you take time out of your life, but with a sense of purpose. You put your trust in your feet, and let your mind move at the same speed as your boots.

'On that first walk, I realised that it allowed me to unconsciously reorganise the filing cabinet of my mind. It felt transformative. On my second journey, I had just come out of a long relationship, and I wanted to figure out how I was feeling. The third was after I'd finished writing a book, and the fourth was to work out the next direction in my career.

'At different times, I walked alone or with friends, but the great joy of a pilgrimage is being surrounded by people doing the same thing. Their purposes might be different, but that community gives you strength and validates your decision. It's a very uplifting experience.'

To Leon, pilgrimage differs from other travel in its search for purpose and meaning. The same route could be a holiday for one person, but a pilgrimage for someone else. It gives you empty space and time, which leads to resolutions and healing.

'I guess an intention helps,' Leon said. 'But I've gone on pilgrimages because I've just been low or confused. The sense of purpose and progress towards a physical destination gives me a sense of simple satisfaction that is hard to find in a world built around abstract notions of success. That, alone, is therapeutic.'

My journey with Dad's ashes may not have had a big physical element to it, but it was certainly a journey to a specific place, with a specific purpose that gave me time to reflect and process my relationship with my father. And it was the outward reflection of an internal journey.

The year before I took Dad's ashes to India, I suddenly and unexpectedly had a panic attack. Without any idea of what was going on, I went to the Accident and Emergency department of a nearby hospital, where a nurse suggested that I visit my GP and talk to them about treatment for depression and anxiety.

The GP had known me all my life, and, rather than prescribing medication, she referred me to a local voluntary counselling service. It changed my life. My counsellor spoke to me about psychological trauma, and explained that it affects how we respond to events that remind us of traumatic experiences in childhood.

I had never suffered physical or sexual abuse, but the counsellor explained that an emotionally abusive parent (which my father was) can have similarly damaging consequences for children. It can lead to anxiety, depression and emotional pain, which we tend to treat by suppressing or changing our feelings, through everything from exercise to substance abuse.

My therapeutic journey helped me find ways to regulate my feelings, while also exploring the underlying trauma that had caused them. Over the course of therapy I came to understand myself better, and became more empathetic to others. Rather than just responding to how I felt about people's behaviour, I began to think about what caused my response, and what might be causing other people to behave as they do. By exploring my trauma through therapy, I gained a greater sense of self-awareness.

Post-traumatic growth (PTG) is the upside of trauma. I say this with a caveat: trauma covers a vast array of experiences, but I hope I don't have to tell you that you should NOT try to traumatise yourself or others to achieve PTG. No one who has gone through trauma would wish it on someone else.

In some circumstances, and with the right recovery, traumatic events can lead to 'growth' that helps us in the future. A simplified version of PTG is this: when we go to the gym and lift weights, we traumatise our muscles. We literally damage them. But if we give them the rest and nutrition that they need while recovering, they will grow back stronger. When Lev and I got lost in Kashmir, it was traumatic, but I learned to be more responsible. And the dopamine-accelerated learning that we experience when scared is a form of PTG.

In *High Risk*, Ben Timberlake describes the Opponent-Process Theory, which is the body's way of countering the effects of something: if you drink alcohol, you feel a relaxed sense of fellowship; the counter-process is a hangover and anxiety. If you do something painful, the counter-process can feel good – such as the runner's high after a challenging run – and if you repeat the exposure enough, it will alter how the body responds to that stimulus.

In the same way, our mind develops mental patterns and frameworks to cope with psychological events. Our responses to psychological trauma can be problematic in normal life – with symptoms ranging from anxiety and depression to violence and substance abuse – but certain experiences and conditions can promote healing in the wake of psychological trauma, leading to PTG, in the form of resilience, empathy, self-awareness and determination.

As I was going through my therapeutic journey, I learned about a form of pilgrimage that people were taking to heal their trauma and achieve PTG. They would travel to the jungles of South America, where they would meet a healer and go through an internal journey with the aid of something called ayahuasca.

Ayahuasca is a brew made from the stems of a vine and the leaves of a shrub. The leaves contain a powerful psychedelic substance called N,N-Dimethyltryptamine (DMT), which naturally occurs in tiny amounts in the brain. The body usually breaks DMT down when it is consumed, but compounds in the vine prevent this from happening, allowing the DMT to enter the bloodstream. The brew is consumed in a ceremonial setting under the guidance of a healer or shaman, and it leads to an incredibly powerful psychedelic experience.

Back in the 1950s and 1960s, psychiatrists and psychologists began experimenting with psychedelics as a way of treating trauma. LSD, MDMA and psilocybin were given to patients at the same time as talking therapy, which seemed to allow them to engage with the underlying trauma without experiencing the negative emotions associated with it. That stands in contrast to more familiar antidepressants, which tend to treat the symptoms of trauma, but not the cause.

Many of these compounds made their way into the counterculture of the 1960s – when they were consumed recreationally – and they were banned. It then became extremely difficult for researchers to continue working with them, and psychedelic-assisted psychotherapy largely disappeared from modern medicine.

While pure DMT itself is a controlled substance, the rules around the plants that are used to brew it are more ambiguous. Indigenous cultures in Peru, Brazil, Colombia and Ecuador have been using ayahuasca for religious and therapeutic purposes for centuries, but it has recently become widely used by people beyond South America, as a way to treat psychological trauma and achieve post-traumatic growth. After hearing about the pilgrimages to South America, I wondered if ayahuasca could contribute to my own psychological healing.

I spent some time researching its risks and benefits, and found an organisation that delivered treatments in Switzerland, where ayahuasca is not criminalised. After speaking to people who had used the same organisation, I completed an online questionnaire and booked a place on an upcoming retreat.

This pilgrimage started around a week before the ayahuasca ceremony, when I began following a specific diet in preparation. I cut out salt, meat, caffeine, alcohol, spices, sugar and dairy products. I also began thinking about my reasons for doing the ayahuasca retreat, and what I wanted to overcome. This alone was incredibly powerful. I felt much more conscious about my behaviours and emotions, and much more vibrant and present.

The ceremony itself took place in February, and I went with a friend who had also become interested in ayahuasca. After landing at Geneva, we picked up a car and headed north towards the mountains. The landscape became more wintery and otherworldly, as if we were heading into Narnia, until we arrived at a chalet that was not unlike a youth hostel. We were met by a Venezuelan psychotherapist named Isamar, Bruno the shaman, and the dozen other people who were doing the ceremony at the same time as us.

After we had settled into our bunks, I headed to the room where we would do the ceremony. Mattresses were placed around the room against the walls, so that we all had our own area, with a space in the middle.

'Ayahuasca is an internal experience,' Isamar said, 'and it is a medicine. It will show you things that could be painful, but which other parts of your psyche need to see. Stay in that experience and listen to what it is trying to tell you. Each of you will have come here for a different reason, but I want you to think about your inner child on your journey. You must see your inner child, embrace him or her, and then never let them go.'

Isamar's words and terminology reassured me because they matched the model of transactional analysis that my counsellor had used during therapy. This describes the different ways that we behave and communicate, based on experiences in childhood. The child ego state is the part of your identity that is the source of emotions; it is fun, playful and creative, but it also learns ways to protect itself from trauma and hurt, and it can behave in a scared or irrational way.

Transactional analysis also models the parent ego state (which is the internalised voice of authority figures from our past) and the adult ego state (which is associated with logical thinking and objectivity). We switch between these states unconsciously when we interact with others, based on our experiences of the past, and sometimes we respond with an inappropriate ego state, which can lead to upset or conflict. By analysing the states and our interactions we can become more conscious of our own beliefs and behaviours.

The idea of throwing all of this in the air, under the experience of a psychedelic compound, was intimidating. But Isamar's words, and the experiences of others – who had achieved positive results through ayahuasca – had given me the resolve that I needed.

'The journey might be confusing,' said Isamar, 'even scary. But the medicine is showing you something important. Tomorrow we will come together for a therapeutic integration session, so that you can make sense of what you experience. Now I shall leave you to your journey.'

The lights were dimmed as the ceremony began. The shaman sat in the middle of the room and we came forward, one by one. First he blew a green tobacco powder called rapé into our nostrils, then we each received a cup of the ayahuasca brew.

I gazed into the unassuming brown liquid and thought about the immensity of what I was about to do: a deep and intense psychedelic dive into my psyche. Once I drank it, there would be no going back, and my life would be changed for ever.

I downed it in one go, and enjoyed the earthy taste of tobacco, liquorice and coffee, then sat back on my mattress.

After around 15 minutes my body began tingling, and I could visualise the ayahuasca coursing through my body. I actually felt the moment that it crossed the blood–brain barrier, and my consciousness exploded.

My body faded away until I was floating in space, where tessellated patterns of triangles, squares and lights played against a background of stars. In front of me, two tunnels appeared. One flashing red, which had a sense of danger and menace to it, and another that glowed blue, and which felt more benign.

I took the blue tunnel and went on a magic carpet ride through the universe, passing colliding galaxies, exploding supernovas and mid-formation solar systems. In the room around me, the shaman was playing music and chanting, and people began 'purging' – vomiting into plastic bags – as the ayahuasca took hold.

All sense of time and identity evaporated as my ego dissolved. One moment I was in my own body, and the next moment I was the man on the other side of the room who was moaning and wailing. Then I was the woman in the corner, laughing and weeping. I tried to wake up, but kept forgetting who I was, and panicked that I would be stuck in this moment for ever. Then my consciousness poured itself back into my body, before the whole thing began again.

When I opened my eyes, it was chaos. People were laughing, then crying, then chattering in nonsensical languages, or being magically transported across the room. The walls and my clothes and my body melted like a Dalí painting, and the only constant was the shaman. He was a being of light, holding dark and dangerous spirits at bay and protecting us from their hungry attempts to reach us.

I began living entire lives of other people: my ancestors in Haridwar; an eagle soaring over the Himalayas; a German soldier in the freezing trenches of the Eastern Front of World War Two. I jumped around the planet, living the lives of Ku Klux Klan racists and Vietnam War peace protestors, cattle farmers on vast open grasslands and gold miners deep beneath the Earth. Thousands of lives that lasted an eternity and no time at all, viscerally experiencing every anxiety, fear and horror that I had ever imagined.

The shaman walked through the room, chanting and blazing light against the horrors, and the room filled with beautiful scents. He played a small wind instrument and waved leaves through the room, and the anxiety and darkness cleared from my mind.

A long, thin rope of golden light appeared before me. It was my love for my mum, my sister and my girlfriend, Dre. I had never wanted to live so much, and to share my life with the people I loved. I pulled my consciousness up the rope until I returned to myself.

My disassociated soul was floating in space again, and I looked down to find myself holding the hand of a younger version of myself. My inner child. My journey through the other lives and horrors and death was a pilgrimage to find him again.

A blue, warm light filled the space, and I was standing with my mum on one side and my dad on the other.

'It will be okay,' they each said in turn. And I knew that it would be.

Behind me was my sister, and Dre, and my counsellor, and all the people I had loved and missed on my journey through forgetting myself. I stepped forward, holding the hand of my inner child, and rose into the sky.

I opened my eyes, and the room made sense again. Tears of joy and love streamed down my face and I went outside, into the cold mountain air. A snow-covered valley stretched before me, lit by the stars. They blazed in the sky above me, more vibrant and colourful than I had ever seen them before, and constellations popped out like the animations of a planetarium.

As the ceremony ended, everyone returned to reality. We all hugged, and I went upstairs to sleep, as dawn crept into the sky.

'Whatever your experience, it was what you needed,' said Isamar. 'Now we will try to make sense of it.'

We were back in the ceremony room for the afternoon integration session. I felt as if my brain had been flossed, put in a blender, and then poured back into my head.

'To reach the light,' she said, 'you have to let the darkness come into you, so you can confront it. You have to clean up the shit and leave it behind you. The defensive measures we developed to cope with trauma have been protecting us, but now they are limitations. Seeing them can be painful, but they are a blessing, and we should be grateful for them. They are the doorway to our potential.'

Isamar worked with the transactional analysis that I was familiar with, but she also talked about more esoteric models related to our family and ancestors.

'We have to take the love and gifts from our family,' she said, 'but we also have to cut some ties with them, or we will be held back. When we have our mother and father behind us, we can move forward.'

As she spoke, I vividly remembered the final phase of my psychedelic experience, where my mother and father were stood either side of me, and I stepped forward with my inner child.

'We need to see our fears and resentment,' continued Isamar, 'or they will grow and consume us.'

Isamar asked two members of the group to represent our mother and our father – a German middle-aged man named Rudi and his wife, Lina. One by one, we had to go up to them and hug them. Men would have to hug Rudi first, and women would hug Lina first. When it came to my turn, I found myself unable to do it.

'Come with me,' Isamar said, leading me towards Rudi, who was becoming my father in my mind's eye.

'Now, tell him what you want to tell him,' Isamar said. I could barely speak, but I looked Rudi in the eye, feeling my emotions flood to the surface.

'I see you,' I said. 'I felt abandoned by you. I acknowledge your burden. And I love you.'

Tears were streaming down my face, and Rudi's. We hugged, in the way that I had never hugged my father, but which I had always wanted.

'I've missed you,' I said, with my head against Rudi's shoulder. 'It's good to see you again.'

And I suddenly felt enormous gratitude towards my father – for meeting my mum, and giving me my life – and I felt compassion for what he had gone through.

I remembered Mum telling me about my Indian grand-father's funeral. Dad was weeping over the casket, wailing that he had never been able to show him what he could do. He never had love or acceptance from his own father, and he never found a way to make peace with that. But through my pilgrimages to India, ayahuasca and therapy, I had found a way to love my father and be grateful to him, without taking on his pain.

For months afterwards, my anxiety receded, and life felt easier. While some of that glow slowly faded, the ayahuasca ceremony unlocked the pain of my relationship with my father, which I have since been able to explore with my counsellor. It started a journey of healing, and it revealed the power of love – for my father, my mother, my sister, and for Dre.

Not all journeys are enjoyable. But the painful ones can sometimes be the most healing.

Chapter 10

WONDER: Heaven in Hokkaido

As my travel writing progressed, and I accumulated a portfolio of published articles, it became easier to pitch to editors and win commissions. With new commissions came new offers of press trips, including one to a place that I had long dreamt of visiting. Japan.

As a child of the 1980s, I was exposed to a surprising amount of Japanese culture. Channel 4 broadcast a different Godzilla film every weekend and my favourite TV show, *Transformers,* was based on a Japanese toy line. But the big jump was the arrival of Nintendo and Sega, which took computer games out of arcades and placed them into our living rooms.

Until then, playing computer games was limited by the coins in my pocket and the patience of my mum. But once computer games could be played at home, innovative genres started to appear, rooted in storytelling and discovery, rather than fast-turnaround thrills.

The game that captured my imagination (and time) was *The Legend of Zelda,* in which I played an unlikely hero trying to save his homeland from an ancient evil. I spent hours exploring caves, castles, mountains and forests, in search of the items and guides that would help me to complete my mission. That sense of limitless discovery was actually more enjoyable than getting to the end of each level.

Zelda designer Shigeru Miyamoto wanted to replicate the sense of wonder that *he* felt as a child while exploring the wilderness around his childhood home. He drew on Japanese myths and landscapes to build the story and its setting, so, when I was offered the press trip to Japan, it felt like I was going on my own *Zelda* quest: to see the land that had inspired my childhood's digital wilderness.

It was autumn when I arrived in the town of Asahikawa, on Japan's northernmost island of Hokkaido. As I drove towards the mountains, I looked down into gorges that transitioned like a rainbow, from green leaves at the bottom, through orange and yellow, to red at higher altitudes. The hazy light deepened on the more distant mountain ranges, making them look turquoise, then blue, then purple and grey.

The top of Mount Asahidake was hidden in cloud, but further down the slopes, jets of white cloud hissed into the air, and the scent of sulphur hit my nose. These broiling fumaroles, heated by underground magma, hinted at the mountain's nature: Asahidake is a stratovolcano.

The top half of the mountain was barren, but the lower slopes featured flashes of colour: red and pink flowers among light green bamboo and dark green dwarf pines. The jagged wound of a side vent ran towards the mountain's peak, filled with steam and yellow patches of sulphur.

Asahidake looked very much like Mount Death, where the

final baddie resides in *Zelda*, and my nostalgia was amplified by the tinkling sound of bells, which accompanied a group of Japanese walkers as they tramped towards the summit.

'It's the bear-bells,' said Kikuo, my guide. 'Brown bears are very shy, and they usually run away when they hear people, but they have been known to attack if they're surprised. The bells let them know you are coming.' She showed me a small brass cowbell, attached to her pack by a piece of leather.

'And this, just in case.' She unclipped a holster and pulled out a canister of pepper spray. 'There's not many bears around Mount Asahidake,' she said, 'but it's a different story in Shiretoko.'

The Shiretoko Peninsula is a few hours' drive from Asahidake and stretches from north-east Hokkaido into the Sea of Okhotsk. In winter its coast is choked by pack ice, which drifts down from the Arctic. For the rest of the year its dark magma cliffs are battered by huge waves, whose hydraulic action squeezes into faults in the rock, widening the cracks until they crumble.

This leaves behind sea-stacks, inhabited by bright green lichen, thin soil, and a few hardy trees. Looking inland, it was barely two miles to the peak of Mount Iō, and the intervening land was a jagged mass of ridges and gullies, coated with a thick forest of birch wood.

'Pioneers tried to farm this peninsula,' said Kikuo, 'but the terrain was too hard, so it was left to run wild. Now it's a national park, and the perfect habitat for bears.'

She led me away from the shore, towards a hollowed-out bowl in the nook of a tree trunk. It was filled with old leaves and resinous bark.

'This is a bear-den,' said Kikuo. 'Probably from last year, by the look of it. They start building them in November, while they fatten up, and they hibernate from December until spring. There will be about ten bears within 400 metres of us right now, but we will have to come back at night to see them, when they go hunting at the river.'

A few hours later we were flashing powerful torches into the darkness, catching the eyes of Ezo owl and deer. We approached a beach on the Iō River, and cautiously looked around, but there was no sign of our quarry.

As we returned to the minibus we spotted a huge salmon lying in the road, its teeth and eyes glinting in the torchlight. The rear part of it was missing, and a line of bright red blood dribbled from its flesh. Our presence must have disturbed a fishing bear, which had silently circled around behind us, then dropped the remains of its dinner as it wandered off into the forest.

The following night, I stayed in a campsite on the shores of Lake Kussharo, which sits in a volcanic caldera. After a barbecue of seafood and vegetables, washed down with plenty of sake, I toddled off to the onsen, hidden along a promontory. These natural hot springs are the more benign manifestation of fumaroles, where gently heated water seeps to the surface and collects in pools.

'Springs are special places,' Kikuo had told me earlier. 'They are a bit magical, and creatures called koro-pok-guru live underneath the plants around them. Koro-pok-guru are like fairies, but naughtier. Gnomes, maybe?'

I saw the steam from the onsen first, in a hollow of gravelly stones, as a mild scent of sulphur and tarmac drifted through the air. After checking for gnomes, I left my robe on a bench, dipped my toes in the water, and then immersed my whole body. My skin tingled at the transition from cold air to intense heat.

It was a clear, moonless, night, and the light from nearby settlements was hidden by the crater rim. The stars were magnificent and, as my eyes adjusted, I could make out their colours. I could even see the dark outlines of interstellar dust against the Milky Way, whose dark shapes were important constellations to the Inca of South America.

As I lay in water heated by the geology of the Earth, looking at starlight that had travelled for millions of years to reach my eyes, my sense of self melted into the grandeur of nature. I was filled with peace and contentment as all my tasks and worries evaporated, replaced by an overwhelming sense of how tiny and temporary my existence was.

I was experiencing 'Awe.'

True awe is a rare and ineffable experience, but I can clearly recall some of the times that I have felt it: that night looking at the stars in Hokkaido; dancing at Glastonbury Festival; watching cremations on the ghats of Varanasi; encountering an elephant in the wilds of Uganda.

Professor Dacher Keltner has been studying awe for decades, and he describes it as *'the feeling of being in the presence of something vast, that transcends your current understanding of the world.'*[41]

Professor Keltner's work is rooted in psychological science's move from 'cognitive' research (which looks at the human mind as a processor of information) to the study of emotions. While most emotions enable the success of individuals, Keltner believes that awe helps us to go beyond our individual selves, to become a valuable part of collective communities.

The context of awe varies across cultures and societies, but Keltner's research identifies consistent sources. He calls them the 'eight wonders of life': moral beauty (the strength, courage and kindness of others); effervescence (collective movement in actions like dance and sport); nature; music; art and visual design; spirituality, religion and mystical encounters; encountering life and death; and big ideas, or epiphanies.

Awe works by quieting our 'default self'. This is the self-conscious, cognitive part of our thinking, which pushes us towards individual goals and achievements, but which also leads to anxiety, depression and self-criticism. The author Aldous Huxley called it 'the interfering neurotic who, in waking hours, tries to run the show'.[42]

During awe, our 'default self' switches off, diminishing those negative feelings and leading to a transcendent state. The boundary between the wider world and our individual selves becomes thinner, and our ego dissolves.

In my experience, each of Keltner's eight sources of awe has a unique flavour and effect: moral beauty in others fills me with admiration, and encourages me to act in the same way; dancing at a festival creates a sense of joy and fellowship, which makes it easier to bond with new friends; while encountering life and death fills me with fear, sadness and reverence, which makes me more appreciative of what I have.

The awe of natural grandeur is of a different order entirely. It evokes a sense of overwhelming insignificance, which changes how I feel about myself and the world around me. It makes me feel small, encourages me to care more about the natural world, and leads to a cognitive shift that puts my worries into perspective.

I wasn't the first person to notice the connection between

nature and profound subjective experiences: nature writers like William Wordsworth, Ralph Waldo Emerson, Henry David Thoreau and Robert Macfarlane have all written about nature's ability to affect us. It doesn't always make us feel good.

The word 'awe' has its roots in the Middle English word 'ege', and Old Norse word 'agi'. Both of them refer to 'dread', 'horror' and 'terror', and there is an echo of these feelings in 'awe'. Our individual insignificance feels particularly acute when we witness the power of an avalanche, or conceive of the vastness of the universe. That insignificance holds a certain terror, which points to awe's associate. The 'Sublime'.

Three hundred years ago, no one chose to visit mountains. They were places of terror and danger, and avoided if at all possible. Just think of how different that is to today, when British families spend their summers in the Lake District or the Highlands, charity fundraisers choose to climb Kilimanjaro and tourists trek to Everest Base Camp.

In *Mountains of the Mind*, Robert Macfarlane investigates why our relationship with mountains changed. In 1688, an Englishman named John Dennis crossed the Alps and wrote about the sense of 'delightful horror' and 'terrible joy' that he experienced while navigating a dangerously narrow pathway. It was triggered by his awareness that with 'a stumble... both life and carcass... [would be] at once destroyed... I was infinitely pleased.'

Seventy years later, the politician–philosopher Edmund Burke tried to conceptualise this powerful emotion. He believed that it imitated the allure of artistic beauty, but was triggered by 'terrible objects', rather than gentle or pretty ones. Burke realised that this emotion – which he called 'the Sublime' – had a distinctive provenance: the terror of potential death.

'Potential' matters here: hanging from a cliff-face by your fingertips will not let you experience the Sublime; but if you stand just close enough to the edge to *imagine* falling off, while actually being perfectly safe, then you might feel a sublime rush.

Burke inspired others, such as the philosopher Jean-Jacques Rousseau, who thought that nature, art and music could be a tonic for the ills of industrialisation. Direct encounters with the Sublime were seen as a pathway to mankind's spiritual salvation, by shattering the suffocation of science and organised religion.

This idea became Romanticism, and it triggered a wave of literature that extolled the virtues of mountains, waterfalls, oceans, thunderstorms, deserts, flora and fauna. The Grand Tourists added places like Chamonix to their itineraries as they searched for the Sublime among the Alps' mountains and glaciers, and it transformed how Charles Darwin perceived our relationship to nature, leading to remarkable insights that shattered mankind's delusion of importance.

The parallel between Burke's 'Sublime' and Keltner's 'Awe' are clear: certain experiences make us aware of the insignificance of our existence, and they come with physiological effects, too. Keltner has shown that awe is associated with goosebumps, the release of feel-good neurochemicals like oxytocin and dopamine, and the stimulation of the parasympathetic nervous system, which helps relax us after high-stress periods.

Dr Annahita Nezami is a psychologist who researches the mental health benefits of wonder, awe and nature, and explores how we can bring them into our lives.

'My PhD explored altered states of consciousness,' she told me. 'I initially looked at near-death experiences, extreme sports and adventures in extreme environments, but I eventually ended up interviewing NASA astronauts about their experience of stargazing in space, and of looking down at the Earth from space. I was particularly interested in the human response to expansive and extraordinary landscapes.

'There was a common theme of "perspective shifts" and "ego dissolution" among these interviewees. They became more ecologically aware, or they began to see the injustices of human activity on a global scale. By physically putting themselves in a more expansive place on the outside, they became more expansive on the inside.

'The ultimate example of this shift in perception after an outward experience is the "overview effect".'

This term was coined by Frank White in the 1980s, to describe the cognitive shift that some astronauts experience after seeing the Earth from space. Frank was working at the Space Studies Institute in Princeton, researching the psychological impact of living in space, and he interviewed retired astronauts about their experience of 'overviewing' our planet.

'I thought that it would just be a perception shift,' Frank told me. 'But those who have experienced the overview effect say that it is beyond words – that you have to experience it to understand it. Different people express it differently, but the words "extraordinary", "transformational" and "awe-inspiring" are often used.

'They realise that there are no real borders or boundaries on our planet, and the things that divide us – politics, race, religion – are all invisible. They see that the atmosphere – which sustains all life on Earth – is incredibly thin, and that the Earth is a whole system where everything is connected to everything else. That creates a sense of unity between the astronaut, and the Earth and its inhabitants.

'But it's not just a cognitive experience. It's emotional. A lot of them talk about spontaneously crying when they first saw our planet from space. They don't know why, and they can't explain it, but the French astronaut Jean-François Clervoy says that it's love. He says, "You love your planet. You've probably been in love, or loved someone or something, and that gives you a hint of the overview effect".'

'Does it lead to a change in beliefs and behaviours?' I asked.

'There's an environmental consciousness that comes with it,' Frank said, 'and a new recognition of the folly of war and conflict. We're on Spaceship Earth, flying through the cosmos, but we are in trouble because the crew – us humans – are not maintaining the ship, and we are not getting along with each other. That's why it's so important to bring the overview effect down to Earth because it can trigger a shift in consciousness, which is vital for us to survive.'

'How could that shift happen?'

'Professional cosmonauts, astronauts and taikonauts go to space for work. They all get the overview of Earth, but the effect differs from person to person. For some, it's a profound spiritual shift, for others it's more subtle. But they all want to communicate it in some way, and some feel an obligation to do so.'

In his book, *Boldly Go: Reflections on a Life of Awe and Wonder*, the *Star Trek* actor William Shatner reflects on his 10-minute flight with the commercial spaceflight carrier Blue Origin, at the age of 90.

'I love the mystery of the universe,' Shatner says in the book. 'Stars exploding years ago, their light travelling to us years later; black holes absorbing energy; satellites showing us entire galaxies in areas thought to be devoid of matter... but when I looked into space, there was no mystery, no majestic awe to behold... all I saw was death. A cold black emptiness... unlike any blackness you can see or feel on Earth. It was deep, enveloping, all-encompassing.

'I turned back toward the light of home. I could see the curvature of Earth, the beige of the desert, the white of the clouds and the blue of the sky. It was life. Nurturing, sustaining, life. Mother Earth. Gaia.'[43]

Shatner had imagined that being above the Earth would give him a sense of connection between all living things and the universe. He instead felt a profound sense of grief at his separation from his home planet, and realised that beauty was down on Earth, rather than beyond it. The contrast between the hostile coldness of space and the nurturing warmth of Earth filled him with sadness and dread at the way in which humans are destroying our home, and the species that live on it.

But it also gave Shatner a sense of hope. That – by being aware of our own insignificance, and the natural grandeur that *makes* us insignificant – we can choose love and life, by dedicating ourselves to caring for our planet and each other.

Not all of us can visit space, of course. But aspects of the overview effect can be achieved without space travel.

'I'll always insist that the pure, high-fidelity definition of the overview effect comes from astronaut experiences,' says Frank, 'but there are adjunct overview effects of different sorts.

'I lived in Germany for three years as a kid, then England for three years of graduate school – that definitely changed my perception of the USA because it let me view my home country from a distance. I've heard from scientists in

Antarctica who believe that they have had a sense of the overview effect because their perception of time and Earth is so different in that environment. Indigenous cultures have always had a more intimate connection to Mother Earth, and they perceive our relationship to nature differently. And a lot of astronauts are mountain climbers and scuba divers – so I think there's something in those activities that alters your perspective.

'And then there's the huge potential of technology.'

Annahita Nezami theorised that the overview effect works by conjuring up awe and other positive emotions. The cognitive dissonance between astronauts' pre-held beliefs and what they see and experience while in space seems to help unlock these positive emotions, and create room for change.

Once she had this model of the mechanism behind the overview effect, Annahita wondered if it were possible to achieve similar outcomes without blasting people into space. She incorporated these ideas into EarthScape VR, which generates aspects of the overview effect through virtual reality-assisted therapies.

'Many eco-psychologists see technology as the root of many problems,' she said. 'But we know that touch, music and visual phenomena can help people to reach transcendent states. I was interested in the direct subjective experiences of the overview effect, and explored whether we could use technology to achieve some of its outcomes without actually going to space.'

In a room at the Royal Society of Arts, I sat down with Annahita and put some VR goggles over my eyes and headphones over my ears. I found myself staring into space, and if I turned my head I could see the arc of the Milky Way, the Moon and the Earth. My ears were filled with the sounds of the Apollo 11 moon landing, ethereal music, a slow heartbeat, and then a female voice preparing me for my voyage by talking about mind–body coherence.

I began moving towards the Moon, which loomed in my visual field, before I raced over the craters of the lunar surface to the horizon, as the Earth rose beyond it. The heartbeat in the headphones sped up, and I felt a wave of vertigo as I left the Moon behind.

The familiar green, white and blue orb of our planet hung against the deep blackness of space, and I floated towards it. A resonant Tibetan chant filled my ears, and the meditative voice told me to look at the cradle of all life. Our home. Earth. A sense of homecoming welled up in my chest and brought tears to my eyes, as I slowly moved into orbit above the Mediterranean, then drifted over the Atlantic, against the movement of the clouds.

For the next 20 minutes, I floated over our planet, guided by the voice, as day turned to night and lights appeared along coastlines. I felt anticipation and dread as storms erupted across the sea, and isolation as I crossed Antarctica, before the aurora australis filled me with joy above the South Pole. Daylight returned as I moved towards the Caribbean and its turquoise waters, before I floated away from Earth once again, and a longing for our home filled my body.

When the visualisation finished I sat in the chair for a minute, then removed the headset and headphones, before speaking to Annahita about my experience.

'Awe comes with an umbrella of positive emotions,' she said, 'as well as physiological effects, such as anti-inflammatory responses. It allows people to step outside of themselves for a sense of expansiveness. There's a reduction in ego, and it's a primer for transcendental states.

'But when we are under chronic stress or in times of adversity, it can be difficult to tap into those positive emotions. Positive psychological therapy allows people to access those emotions, so that they can revisit them more sustainably. The VR is a tool to aid that, and we build on it with therapies and workshops. That helps clients to integrate the experience, and achieve shifts in perspective, which can have a positive impact on their mental health.

'Awe is also a gateway to contemplation and consideration. We are all consumed by our daily challenges, but if we can create awesome experiences, it opens the door to unity and cohesion.'

Annahita believes that there are different typologies of awe, and the most extreme version overwhelms you with an unfathomable mix of trepidation and fear. It matches Burke's concept of the Sublime.

'The awe we aim to elicit in the VR is closer to the Sublime,' she said. 'It's quite acute, but awe can also inspire wonder, which is more prolonged, and connected to curiosity. Wonder is more cognitive, rather than the visceral, felt experience of awe.

'Humans come from a long history of nomadism. There is a part of us that requires exploration and movement, and travel is tied up with awe, and curiosity, and wonder. This complex mix of emotional, psychological and physiological reactions is not only good for our own mental health, but it can help foster a sense of connection with others.'

Professor Keltner believes that awe evolved through natural

selection, so that social mammals could cope with novel threats and cooperate as communities. It encourages problem-solving, inspiration and creativity, and he agrees with Annahita that, 'Wonder – the mental state of openness, questioning, curiosity, and embracing mystery – arises out of experiences of awe.'

It's tempting to believe that we can only attain awe and wonder through travel. After all, I experienced the awe of nature in Hokkaido, the awe of life and death in Varanasi, and the awe of visual design at the Taj Mahal. Each of these experiences had an enduring effect, which made me think about the world differently. But Keltner believes that true wonder comes from seeing the awesome in the mundane.

Kids find awe in everything, but they are particularly fascinated with nature – bugs, rain, puddles, trees, animals – because it is their playground for developing physical, cognitive and social skills. Keltner believes that biophilia (the tendency to seek connection with nature) is an innate trait that aids this exploration. That love of nature is often suppressed in our city-dwelling lives, but it can be reawakened through cultivation and practice.

When I return to London after spending a few days in the countryside, I notice that my mood has lifted. That emotional shift also triggers a cognitive shift, and I start to pay attention to the bark of trees on my street, or the changing colour of their leaves. I become filled with a sense of wonder that makes me seek more mundane awesomeness, like the phases of the Moon or the colour of clouds.

So perhaps it's not the *things that we experience* during travel that *generate* awe but the *mindset that we create* during travel that *enables* awe. And just as novelty – which I experienced during the rugby tour to New Zealand – triggered my latent curiosity, being exposed to awe can trigger our latent wonder.

Wonder requires cultivation and practice. But the rewards are awesome.

Travel journalism has made me better at paying attention to things because they become the details in my articles: architecture, trees, animals, clothes, art, music, food, drink, accents, turns of phrase, history and weather have all become my measures of reality.

We notice things when they are unusual. The tone of a Dutch police siren, or the font of a French number-plate, stands out because it is different to what we see or hear at home. But as I started to spend more time travelling with work, I began to see *home* itself through this lens because everything was unusual.

Elements of wonder began creeping into the apparently mundane: I found myself stopping on Waterloo Bridge, admiring how the dome and stone of St Paul's Cathedral contrasts with the metal and concrete of the City; I sat on the top deck of double-decker buses, enjoying views into spaces that are hidden from ground level; I took time to appreciate tiled murals in Underground stations; I listened to buskers performing in public spaces.

Nature played its part, too. As the year progressed, I noticed the development of trees along my street, from bare branches to buds, blossom and seeds, before their final flush of autumn colours. I put an app on my phone that allowed me to identify plants, bushes and birdsong, and I dashed out to the countryside to forage for blackberries and chestnuts.

The poet T S Eliot wrote,

Why We Travel

And the end of all our exploring
Will be to arrive where we started
And know the place for the first time.

Perhaps that was starting to happen to me. I enjoyed being home, and some of my earlier urges to see every corner of the planet were slowly diminishing. Not just because I had visited many of the places I had wanted to, but because home seemed so much richer to me than it ever had before.

Even if we don't travel regularly, we can trick ourselves into seeing home in a new light. In my final year of university, I visited a friend who lived near Angel tube station. At the end of the night I decided to walk back to Waterloo station, to catch the first train home. This was long before smartphones, and I had no objective for the walk, so I just followed my nose and my curiosity.

It led me past butchers finishing their morning shift at Smithfield Market. I turned a corner and saw St Paul's Cathedral up close for the first time. And I watched the sun rise behind an empty Tower Bridge. It was all fairly mundane, but it was wonderful because I paid attention and noticed it.

But now that I live in London – and mostly commute between its different boroughs for a specific purpose – I often find myself moving through the city on autopilot.

Back in Chapter 4, we met the twentieth-century Parisian intellectuals who began thinking about different ways to journey around their city. 'Psychogeography' looks at how the built environment affects the emotions and behaviour of individuals, and a group known as Situationist International developed a mindset for drifting around the city, in an 'unorganised and aimless, yet significant, walk'. This style of

213

movement, called dérive, was intentionally reactionary and playful, moving around and about, rather than from place to place. By moving on foot, revelling in chance encounters and thinking about travel in a new way, these Parisians tried to reveal 'marvels buried in the everyday'.[44]

I prefer to use psychogeography more consciously, by forcing myself to observe in a new way. An easy hack for this is to look out for very specific things as you walk – such as the colour red. When I do this, I find my eye drawn to things that I might otherwise miss, ranging from clothes in storefronts or furniture in houses, to architectural flourishes and street art. In doing so, the city comes to life, and I find myself delighted by the surprise of new discoveries.

My work in radio and podcasts has made me think about sound in new ways, too. It's an aspect of the environment that shapes how we feel, but it usually sits outside our conscious awareness. Try using the voice notes app on your phone, to capture specific sounds along a journey. This will bring sound right to the forefront of your awareness, and help you to understand how sounds change with your surroundings.

Stories are another way to change how we perceive our surroundings. As we saw in Chapter 1, I recently walked between locations in London that are associated with William Shakespeare. In doing so, I built a creative new pathway for myself through the city, delving behind offices and warehouses to find a particular site or feature. Because I was looking for hints of Elizabethan London, I noticed the decoration of buildings and the contemporary legacy of historical boundaries. That allowed me to see the city in a new light – as layers of history and culture, and not just an environment to pass through.

In his book *Walk the Lines,* Tube fanatic Mark Mason walked the entire London Underground network at surface level. He followed the routes of the tube – places that we normally whizz beneath in the dark – to see neighbourhoods that we normally ignore, and to understand what ties them together. The walk was a creative way to explore the city differently, but it also had a more philosophical impact on Mason.

'My love of walking the lines,' he said to the Dabbler Book Club, 'wasn't just a love of London, or of exercise, or of achieving a goal; it was a love of life. Looking forward to a journey, planning it and marking it off, is a subconscious substitute for the thing we can't do, namely controlling our life. Relishing a journey in the memory is the equivalent of immortality, or at least reincarnation.'

The greatest modern psychogeographer is Alastair Humphreys, whose 'microadventures' conjure up freedom between the end of one workday and the beginning of the next. My favourite example is catching a train out of London, camping on a hill overnight, and then heading back home the following morning. I'm always astonished at how rewarding this simple act is, and it makes me see the opportunity for adventure in places that I usually overlook. For his latest book, *Local,* Alastair spent a year exploring the 400 square kilometres around his house with a single map, to remind us that nature and wildness are closer than we think.

What connects these techniques of travel – from unusual walking routes to hacking how we notice things – is 'the un-expected': chance encounters, accidental discovery and the often-overlooked. Through them, we attain the cognitive experience of wonder, and the emotional experience of awe.

*

215

Dan Kieran's approach to travel stems from a dislike of flying. In his book, *The Idle Traveller*, he notes that many people complain about the stress and hassle of air travel, and it amazes him that they choose to miss out on some of the most interesting and fun parts of travel.

'Now that we can move so quickly around the world,' he says in the book, 'most of us don't actually travel any more – we only arrive. I take the slower route if I can because it gives the journey and the places I visit a much greater sense of meaning. Travelling slowly changes the way my mind interprets the world.'[45]

Kieran recounts his experience of taking the Eurostar to Paris, as against travelling there by plane. As the train took him from Kent and into northern France, he noticed the similarities in the landscape on both sides of the Channel, as well as the subtle differences in infrastructure or the way that fields were laid out. By arriving in Paris at a train station in the city centre – rather than at a remote airport – he entered a space designed for locals, rather than one that encouraged him to behave like a tourist, and it made him feel much more comfortable.

This echoes my own fondness for slow travel. When we are freed from the constraints of aeroplanes and airports, we experience the world at a more digestible pace, and we become more likely to meet locals. During my journey along the New Iron Curtain, I mostly travelled by train, and I was astonished at how often my fellow passengers shared their food and drink, told me their family history or offered me a place to stay. That has never happened on a plane, where an instinctive barrier goes up between neighbours, and the journey feels like a chore to overcome.

In his book, Kieran explores two concepts of time, which are named for the ancient Greek gods that looked after it. The first is Chronos: the scientific, measurable time that most of us are familiar with (and which gives us words like chrono-logical). The other is Kairos: 'divine time'; moments that seem pregnant with potential that can change your life for ever, like Sir Chay Blyth's opportunistic moment.

Kairos represents the type of time that most of us want in our travels; but holidays are bound by the discrete, diminishing time of Chronos, with a series of activities and diversions to tick off. It's a more mortal form of time because we know it will run out, and that creates its own sense of anxiety.

The transcendent state of awe, where we feel present in the moment, takes us into Kairos. Slow travel helps us get there because it eliminates itineraries and gives us the time and space for wonder and serendipity. That's also why I tell my mates to revisit places: if they've previously done everything that they *should* do, then they won't feel guilty about doing what they *want* to (such as wandering around aimlessly).

Travel journalism is inherently 'Kairos-y' because it forces me to travel with purpose and wonder. By asking questions, I find new things to be curious about, and new leads to follow. Each moment is an opportunistic moment – conjuring up possibilities – and plans go out the window as I discover new people to speak to, and new paths to follow.

Not only is the experience of awe unlike anything else we encounter, but certain flavours of awe – particularly the Sublime – can change the very way that we think and feel about the world.

Travel allows us to encounter transcendent states of awe – when we stand on the side of a mountain, or look up at the

Milky Way – and it develops the cognitive quality of wonder. This is a positive feedback loop: by tapping into wonder, and seeing the world in new ways, we become more consciously aware, and awe finds new routes into our lives. As does another emotion. Love.

Chapter 11

EROTICISM: The Blue Zone

Most of my travel has been done alone. Even when I've travelled with others, I've only really had my own motivations to consider.

That changed when I met Andrea Jayne Thompson (Dre) at a friend's charity event, and she asked me out for a drink. I liked her boldness (and unwillingness to adhere to gender stereotypes) and we began dating. We also shared a love of travel, and I overcame my lack of cash by wrangling some press trips to Turkey and Switzerland. They became the template for a more ambitious adventure: driving from Seattle to San Diego, and then spending a week in Costa Rica.

Dre had been practising as a photographer, and a few of her images had already been published with my articles, so I managed to secure some newspaper commissions that covered both of our costs. The downside of this remarkable deal was that I had a lot of stories to research, and a lot of content to generate.

To me, this was second nature. Going abroad was at the core of my work, so I found it hard to think of travel as a holiday. Dre, meanwhile, was a doctor who was undertaking intense training as a surgeon, so three weeks away from work was a big deal. She wanted to return home refreshed and relaxed, while still making the most of the places that we saw.

That led to inevitable friction. In places like Big Sur, I wanted to push on, to do interviews and gather information for my articles; Dre wanted to sit on a beach and read a book. When we visited a town, I wanted to go to a museum, or interview some minor celebrity; Dre wanted to enjoy a long lunch.

We talked through our individual motivations during a hike in Yosemite National Park, and we figured out a way to travel together: at the end of each day – or before each segment of a trip – we talked through what each of us wanted, and worked out what was needed for the commissions. Then we made a plan, which sometimes involved spending time by ourselves, and sometimes meant both of us doing things that we would never have otherwise chosen to do.

We discovered that this improved both of our travelling experiences because it meant adding new things to our travels, rather than merely compromising. Dre turned out to be an excellent journalistic companion, who noticed things that I would have missed and asked questions that I would not have thought of. Through that – and her encouraging me to actually relax while abroad – my experience of travel was altered, and our relationship deepened.

Esther Perel is a psychotherapist who grew up in Belgium, trained partly in Israel, and works and teaches in the United

States. She specialises in relationships, and much of her career has been devoted to understanding sex and desire in committed relationships.

'Familiarity is reassuring,' she says in her book *Mating in Captivity,* 'And it brings a sense of security. But we want the aliveness and excitement of the beginning of a relationship.'[46]

For Perel, the key is maintaining 'eroticism,' which she describes as that 'quality of aliveness, a pathway to freedom – not just the narrow definition of sex that modernity has assigned to it.'

'Eroticism thrives in the space between the self and the other,' she says, 'It requires separateness. The challenge for modern couples lies in reconciling the need for what's safe and predictable with the wish to pursue what's exciting, mysterious and awe-inspiring.

'With too much distance there can be no connection. But too much merging eradicates the separateness. When people become fused – when two become one – connection can no longer happen. There is no one to connect with.'

So what does this have to do with travel?

I believe that this loss of eroticism can happen in our relationship with travel itself. When travel becomes familiar or routine, it loses the mysterious 'aliveness' that we found in our first adventures. Planes become boxes that take us between places, rather than a chance to gaze out of the window. After a few stomach upsets, we become less willing to try new foods. So, over time, we take fewer risks, but that makes our experiences less memorable and less meaningful.

We have to work at erotic travel. I don't mean sex tourism. I mean erotic in Perel's definition. Eroticism is playfulness, novelty, spontaneity and wonder – all of which are essential to good travel. Try new foods. Go to new places. Make yourself uncomfortable.

In the context of a relationship, travel can also be a pathway to spontaneity and playfulness, by getting us out of the groove of familiarity. Each partner could plan part of a trip, without asking the other for approval. That allows us to reveal interests that we normally hide out of embarrassment, and it encourages our partner to try new things. By taking it in turns to surrender responsibility – and your right to complain if you don't like it – you can find a sense of playful creativity.

'Blue Zones' are regions of the world with populations that regularly live into healthy old age. There are just five Blue Zones on the entire planet, and research suggests that they are caused by a combination of factors, which range from diet and weather to religion. A magazine had commissioned me to find out why Costa Rica was home to one of these exceptional regions, so Dre and I flew there from California.

From the town of Puerto Viejo, on Costa Rica's Caribbean coast, we took a dug-out canoe up the Yorkin River, deep into the jungle that borders Panama. This is the homeland of Costa Rica's indigenous Bribri people, whose remoteness kept their culture alive during successive European invasions.

The jungle is teeming with life, and the Bribri use that bounty for everything, ranging from camphor sap that repels mosquitoes to a plant that they chew for toothache. To my untrained eye the Bribri gardens looked much like the rest of the jungle, with different species piled around each other and butterflies flitting between the branches. But that apparent chaos was deceptive.

'That's because you are used to seeing farms of single crops,' said Albin, a local guide. 'We don't farm monocultures because the plants evolved to work in harmony: the legumes put nitrogen in the soil, and banana trees put down potassium, so we don't need artificial products or fertilisers.

'Each plant attracts different birds, so there's hundreds of bird species here, while you might find only a dozen on a monoculture farm. Each species eats different insects, and there are also coral snakes and boas that kill rodents, so we don't need pesticides or traps.'

'What about venomous snakes?' asked Dre.

'We do kill the fer-de-lance and bushmaster snakes,' Albin said. 'Our gardens are right next to our villages, and those snakes can be really dangerous, especially to curious kids. Or curious tourists.'

The boat pulled in to a small stone beach. Two young children – a brother and sister, watched over by their dad while he fished – giggled and screamed as they jumped into the river. They let the current carry them to an overhanging branch, which they used to haul themselves back to the riverbank, before running upstream to repeat the whole process.

The air was filled with the stony smell of river water, and the warm sweetness of flowers and grasses. As we walked towards the village, Albin plucked fruits from the trees, most of which were completely unfamiliar to me.

'This is a water apple,' he said, before taking another. 'This is monkey fruit. And that one is starfruit. They look different from the ones you'd find in a supermarket because they are less hybridised.'

He approached a tree that was about 20 feet tall and had fruits sprouting directly from the trunk and branches. They were shaped like a ribbed rugby ball about the length of my handspan, and mostly yellow or green.

'This is the cacao tree,' said Albin, tenderly touching the trunk. 'Our mythology says that it was the most beautiful tree in paradise and that it came to Earth as a gift. Before Europeans came, we even used the seeds as currency.'

He plucked a yellow fruit, dappled with orange, and knocked it against the trunk. It split in half to reveal white flesh and perfectly tessellated seeds.

'The flesh is sweet,' he said, handing me a seed to suck on, 'but the seed is bitter before it is prepared.'

We entered a clearing of thatched houses on stilts, and a white wooden hut that looked like a large birdhouse. Inside were racks of cacao seeds, now coloured red and brown.

'The seeds are removed from the fruit,' he said, 'and left to ferment for a week. That's when the chocolate flavour develops, thanks to enzymes and microorganisms. Then we dry them in the sun for five days.'

I picked up one of the shrunken seeds and bit into it. It was still bitter, but it now had the distinctive taste of chocolate. Albin grabbed a handful and tossed them in a pan, which he heated on a stove. After a few minutes, he broke the seed's outer shell and pulled out the toasted inner flesh, which is called the 'nib'. It tasted of bitter chocolate, mellow coffee and chestnuts.

The toasted seeds were rolled with a stone, then tossed to separate the lighter shell from the heavier nibs, which Albin poured into a hand grinder. As he turned a handle, thick paste oozed from the bottom of the grinder and the deep, rich scent of dark chocolate filled the hut.

This was pure cacao butter, filled with flecks of toasted nibs.

The Bribri dry it and sell it to tourists and, when added to condensed milk, it creates the best chocolate that I have ever eaten.

'It has taken vision to bring tourism to this area,' said Albin. 'But it's the only way to keep our culture alive.'

'Why?' I asked.

'Ever since Europeans came here,' he said, 'we Bribri have been under pressure. Now the government wants to build dams and ask us to give up our land, for "the good of the country", and for an enormous fee. But our people already gave everything to the invaders. Where has that gotten us? All we have is our land, and our traditions. And our cacao.

'In a few years, the dam will be forgotten, and more energy needed, and new rivers dammed, and the jungle turned into banana plantations. But this village and this culture will be gone for ever. Tourism forces people to notice us. And, through the story of our cacao, people learn the story of our people.

'It is strange. Cacao was important to our ancestors. It was a sacred plant that made us strong – not just physically, but spiritually. Now it's one of the reasons tourists come, and that might be what saves us from development.'

'Does chocolate make Costa Rica a Blue Zone?' asked Dre.

'If it's made like this,' said Albin, 'then chocolate can be a superfood. Full of antioxidants and flavonoids, which reduce inflammation. It can help to prevent cancer, and it also has esoteric, spiritual properties for our people.

'But a healthy life comes from many things: community; a sense of purpose; being outdoors; an active lifestyle. And good healthcare, of course, which is difficult in these remote communities. But, actually, not all of Costa Rica is a Blue Zone. To find the true Blue Zone, you have to go to Nicoya.'

That night, as we lay in our hammocks above the trees, Dre and I began planning the next step of our journey.

'I'd never have come to this village if I was just coming on a holiday,' she said, 'but it's such an incredible experience being in this beautiful place and finding out about the culture first hand. Asking questions, meeting fascinating people... it feels like such a privilege. Thank you for bringing me along.'

Nicoya is on the opposite side of Costa Rica from the land of the Bribri, on a peninsula that juts into the Pacific. Nicoya's indigenous Chorotegan culture has more in common with the Mesoamericans of Mexico than with the Bribri of the jungle because of the geography of Central America. The clearest legacy of this is in the food: the roadsides of Nicoya were filled with cobs of yellow and purple maize, drying in the sunshine, just like you would find in Mexico.

'The Blue Zone is a real thing,' said Ezekiel Aguirre Perez, a traditional Chorotegan potter living in the town of Mutambu. 'Around here, people regularly live into their eighties and nineties, and that's without access to regular healthcare. They don't take vitamins and so on. Instead, their very way of being is healthy.'

Blue Zone researchers have identified the importance of diet, with an emphasis on lots of vegetables and a low consumption of meat. In Nicoya, maize is used in everything, from patties to soups. It is fermented into chica and chicheme alcoholic beverages, or roasted and ground into Piñol, which makes a drink like malted Horlicks. The Chorotega also have a strong sense of community, with the whole town coming together to build each new house. It's a concept called 'mano vuelta', which roughly translates as 'work for the collective benefit'.

'People look for tricks to live longer,' Ezekiel said, 'but you can't live a life of consumption and greed, then balance it out with superfoods. You have to live in an integrated way: an active life; a kind life; a community life.

'When someone in the village needs a new house, we all come together and build it. When someone slaughters a pig, we all come together and share it. No one eats too much, but we all have enough. And we take it in turns to provide.'

Ezekiel told us about a man called Pachito who lived nearby, and who had recently celebrated his hundredth birthday. He gave us the address and suggested that we pay him a visit.

Pachito's hacienda sat in a shallow valley surrounded by flowering bushes. Ezekiel had called ahead and told him we were coming, but we had to wait with Pachito's granddaughter until he came back because he was out visiting friends.

We were not waiting for long. Pachito trotted down the driveway on his white horse, which he tied up in the back garden before deftly dismounting. As he walked in, he gave me a firm handshake, but pulled Dre in for a kiss on the cheek.

'Such a charmer,' she laughed. He responded with a wink, and settled down in a chair.

'Sorry for my delay,' he said. 'I had to go and visit a friend of mine who wasn't feeling too well – but he is 102, so what can you expect?'

'Do you ride every day?' I asked.

'When I'm still, things start to ache,' he said. 'I've worked all my life as a sabanero – a cowboy – so it's more natural to me than walking. I never did any kind of separate exercise, but it's a very active life.'

Pachito sat down on a low wicker chair, with pictures of his many descendants on the wall behind him. His granddaughter handed him a cup of warm Piñol, kissed him on the head, and then headed out to the garden.

'This was never a region of education and wisdom,' Pachito said, 'but it was always a place of hard work. The biggest difference from today is that we knew where our food came from. We grew rice and maize, raised cattle and pigs, and kept chickens, which fed on our food scraps. It wasn't a great assortment, but it was pure and healthy, and we ate three times a day. That's enough.'

'And what do you think is important, Pachito?' I asked. 'What do you tell your children, and great-grandchildren, and great-great-grandchildren?'

'During my life,' he said, 'I was not a grand person – a person of significance, or anything like that – but I have always been a good friend. You have to love yourself, and others. Because if you love a friend, you cannot wish anything bad on other people. That stops things going bad for you from the inside.'

As we left, he patted my hand and nodded towards Dre. 'And it's very important to love a good woman,' he said.

Dre and I finished our trip at the southern end of the Nicoya Peninsula, which is popular with backpackers and surfers. We stayed in a lodge made of bamboo, which had an outdoor shower, and a terrace that looked over the ocean.

Rather than planning our days, we let our mood and serendipity guide us. We took zipline rides through the forest canopy, ate ceviche from beach shacks, danced to soca in bars (badly, in my case), and tried our hand at surfing (again, badly in my case). I even sat on the beach and read.

By travelling with Dre, I was finding new things to enjoy about travel. It was challenging to consider someone else's needs when I was so used to travelling only for my own whims, but it helped to deepen our communication, and our consideration of each other. It gave us the space to develop our relationship, and to shake out the familiar mindset of home. It was good.

There is a constant psychological tension between individual and shared goals, just as there is a tension between the freedom of solo travel and the joy of sharing travel with others. This reflects the tension between our imagined concept of the world and the world as we actually experience it.

We naturally compare our lives to an impossible, imagined, perfect version – drawn from television, advertising and social media – which can make it hard to enjoy the present. In *The Idle Traveller*, Dan Kieran suggests that travel's displacement of comfort, routine and place can give us the chance to explore this tension. By taking our minds off autopilot to deal with the unfamiliar, our conscious mind comes to the fore.

We seem more willing to share our hopes and fears with friends (or even strangers) when we meet them on the road, and Kieran wonders if this could explain why people 'find themselves' while travelling. It opens up a space to start conversations because we 'are more conscious of the experience of being alive.'

He believes that the key lies in 'changing our perception of the world', and it draws on three key tenets: following a hunch that a journey is the right thing to do; travelling slowly; and relying on the kindness of strangers. It's the opposite of 'sightseeing', which involves arriving somewhere, 'doing' everything in a guidebook and seeing the locals as obstacles to overcome.

Kieran reflects on an interview with the travel writer Paul Theroux, who believes that, if you travel with someone you know, you will constantly be pulled back into your usual mindset. When you are alone, the backdrop of an unfamiliar place disrupts the 'default self' that we met in Chapter 10. Your identity slips away, and you 'explore often-neglected parts of yourself'.

My own experience of solo travel seems to back up Kieran's hypothesis, particularly when I leave a lot of open space in my itinerary. As well as exploring a place, it allows me to explore my relationship with myself.

Solo travel can help us to maintain our vital 'separateness' (in Esther Perel's model) by giving time to those parts of ourselves that we normally turn off or turn down. That might be doing activities that we know our partner is scared of, or eating foods that they dislike, or going to museums that would bore them. This doesn't require weeks of solo travel – a day trip or overnighter can help you to foster your individuality.

Being physically separated from our partner can also remind us of what we take for granted. It gives us the chance to miss each other.

In late 2019, I travelled to Nevada for a festival called Burning Man. As a veteran attendee of British festivals, I thought I knew what I was letting myself in for, but Burning Man was unlike anything else I had previously encountered.

British music festivals are all about the music. Your ticket gets you a line-up of bands and singers on big stages, which you watch in various states of inebriation, alongside thousands of other people. You camp in a field and pay for your food and drink, and then you go home, as a clean-up crew sorts out the mess that's left behind.

Burning Man is an anarchic take on that model. You pay

for your ticket, but you don't know what you are going to get. It's in the middle of the Black Rock Desert, and you have to take all of your supplies with you. You can't spend money once you're inside Burning Man, but the flip side is that everything is free once you are there because every attendee brings something to give away.

DJs set up sound stages and moving disco-trucks. Mechanics and welders build huge art-cars, which they drive around for the enjoyment of other 'Burners' (as the attendees call themselves). People spend an entire year preparing kitchens and bars, where Burners can wander up and receive everything from beers to margaritas, and from ramen to barbecue, without doing anything in return. The only catch is that there are no bins, so everyone has to take out everything that they bring in.

There are tents of 'trance yoga' sessions, acrobatics and meditation. A giant car wash, where hundreds of naked people have the desert's dust washed off by cheerleaders and firefighters. People take part in ultra-marathons and beer-carrying football games. Teachers deliver classes on everything from 'Radical Consent' and 'The Art of Kissing' to 'Lightsabre Combat Training' and 'Cosmic Journeying'. There's even an 'Orgy Dome'.

The site is vast. The only way to get around is on bicycles, and surreal recommendations fly around at the speed of rumour: 'DJ X is playing at the stage next to The Pyramid, behind The Space Shuttle. Start time is the second burning of The Fortress after sunset.' Once night falls, the brown and grey of the desert gives way to the psychedelic shapes and colours of neon-lit art-cars. Circus performers in lurid monster suits stomp around on stilts.

It was like a blend of *Mad Max* and an ayahuasca trip, and it actually led me to ayahuasca-like introspection.

I had gone with a couple of close friends, and our days were spent wandering between installations and workshops that provoked deep thinking. We shared our hopes and fears. We expressed our love for each other, and our resentments. We danced to great music and we encountered incredible art, but something was missing. I wished that I was sharing it all with Dre.

One evening – having spent the entire day drinking craft beer in a Western-themed saloon bar with a group of Hollywood stunt actors – I suddenly got signal on my mobile phone. I proceeded to send Dre every photo of us together, telling her how much I missed her. In hindsight, this probably didn't communicate the romantic sentiment that I meant it to, but at least Dre saw the funny side.

'Wow,' she said in her message the next morning. 'That's quite something! At least I know you like me.'

I realised that I wanted to share the rest of my life with her, so I began thinking about how I would make that happen. But Dre got there first.

A few weeks after I returned from Burning Man, she suggested that we go for a walk up Parliament Hill – my favourite viewpoint in London – and over to a pub in Highgate. We were both running a little late, so it was already dark by the time we met, and it started to rain as we traipsed up the hill. As we looked out at the city from the summit, Dre turned to me.

'I really enjoy my life with you,' she said. 'You show me new things, and we have lots of fun, and I think we have a lot of shared values.'

'I enjoy our life together, too,' I said.

'Well, I think we should do it for a lot longer.'

'Me too.'

'Good.'

Dre then got down on one knee, in the mud, pulled out a small box and said, 'Ashwin Colin Bhardwaj, will you marry me?'

I looked down, astonished, and blurted out, 'I was supposed to do this!'

'Is that a yes?'

'Yes!'

'Great!'

She then placed the ring (which was shaped like the face of a bear) on my left hand, got up and kissed me. Then she pulled a bottle of champagne out of her bag, and we drank it at the top of the hill, before we called our families to tell them the good news.

From *Wild* to *Eat Pray Love*, there are plenty of books that extol the benefits of travelling alone. But are we ignoring the potential benefits of travelling with others? It might take a bit more work, but could travelling with others allow us to explore the 'often-neglected parts' of our relationships, *and* of the places that we visit?

As my friend Levison Wood once said, 'The hardest part of any journey is getting to the start line. But then there's still the rest of the journey to complete. All the obstacles and challenges. All the unexpected events and opportunities. The joys and the sorrows. That's the bit you remember.'

Relationships are much the same. While most fairy tales finish with the wedding, I found my wedding to Dre to be just the next step in a journey. Travel was central to the evolution of our relationship, and it continues to play a part in how we spend time together. It's been a way for us to excite and surprise each other, but it's also led to our biggest frustrations and even arguments.

Travelling with others can deepen our relationships, and help us to experience the world in new ways. Other people make us see, eat, drink, and do things that we never would on our own. Sometimes we enjoy it, but sometimes we hate it. If nothing else, that reveals new things about our own character.

Eroticism fades when risk is replaced by reassuring familiarity. That can happen with our love of travel, as well as our love of each other. It is tempting to plan our itinerary in line with 'The Top Ten Restaurants in This City', Instagram influencers or reviews on Tripadvisor. But that creates expectation, which might be disappointed, and it shuts off our pathways to freedom. If we give up some control, then that sense of adventure returns.

We can go even further and surrender to chance itself. Roll a dice to decide if you will go left or right at a junction. Pick a card from a pack to decide how many restaurants you will pass before you stop. Who knows what you will find? It could be awful, or it could be wonderful. But it will definitely be playful, creative, and exciting.

It will be erotic.

Chapter 12

HOPE: Mountains of Mortality

2019 to 2021 were a big couple of years. The world locked down with Covid. Russia prepared to invade Ukraine. Dre and I got married. My sister, Barty, got married. And my mum was diagnosed with ovarian cancer, and passed away.

I'm writing these words on the second anniversary of Mum's passing, and I can feel myself disassociating as my brain tries to protect me from the anguish of her loss. Most days I am okay. But sometimes I realise that I will never see Mum again, nor tell her what I have been up to, nor see her cuddle my baby. Then my grief bursts out of every pore in my body, leaving me unable to do anything but mourn and seek distraction through any means.

Mum was diagnosed two days after Dre proposed to me. From one of our happiest moments as a family, to one of the most devastating. Unlike the breast cancer that Mum had overcome a decade earlier, this cancer could only be managed, not cured. What mattered changed immediately. Every day with her was precious. Every WhatsApp message cherished.

She was just starting to enjoy life, having recently retired, and it was our turn to look after her, rather than the other way round. So it seemed extra cruel that this freedom was met with cancer and Covid.

Mum approached death in a truly remarkable way: by focusing on living life, rather than being bitter about its loss. Between lockdowns and chemotherapy, she filled her world with joy: we spent days in the garden with family, visited cafés and restaurants with friends, and arranged little trips away. She had always been the most grateful and joyous person that I have ever known, and she relished every moment of her remaining time.

Just a few weeks after a long stay in hospital due to the adverse effects of chemotherapy, Mum made a remarkable temporary recovery, in time for Barty's wedding to her Australian boyfriend, Blake. She looked fabulously radiant, and made a beautiful speech, on what she described as 'the happiest day of my life'. She spent the whole evening dancing with Barty's friends, who she had known for over 20 years.

Mum's maternal family came from Chester, and she had spent the first few years of her life there. We had often spoken about visiting, so just after Barty's wedding, Mum and I took a trip to the city.

As we drove north, Google Maps kept switching its recommended route because of traffic. The knot of motorways around Birmingham is confusing at the best of times, and I missed our exit, adding 40 minutes on to our journey. I cursed, annoyed that I was wasting our precious time in traffic, but Mum was completely serene.

'Don't worry, Ashy B,' she said, 'I'm sure it will all work out for the best.'

She was right. We took the next exit into glorious country-side, and headed towards the city of Wrexham in North Wales. The mountains of Eyri Snowdonia National Park loomed on the horizon, and the roadsides were ablaze with the purple and yellow of flowering rhododendron and laburnum.

'Isn't this wonderful,' Mum said, 'and just to think, if we had taken the right exit, we would have missed it.'

During her stay in hospital, Mum had lost a lot of weight, and she was now making the most of her new-found appetite. We stopped at a service station that happened to have a KFC, and ordered some fried chicken.

'This is delicious!' Mum said. 'I can't believe I've never had it before. Let's get a sundae, too!'

We stayed in Chester city centre, in a red-brick terraced house like the one Mum grew up in. She was using a walking frame to get around, but still carried herself with a sense of effortless style, wearing a navy-blue kimono dress, with a purple scarf thrown round her neck. As we walked along a shopping street of timber-framed buildings, two young women approached her.

'Can I just say that I love your outfit?' one of them said. 'You look absolutely fabulous!'

Mum beamed back, 'Oh, thank you. You two look pretty snazzy, too.'

It was to be her final summer. Just two weeks after mine and Dre's wedding she was admitted to Thames Hospice, a beautiful place on the outskirts of Windsor, overlooking a lake near the river.

'I've had my name down since they built it,' she joked. 'I'd much rather pass away here than in some noisy hospital with people prodding and poking me every hour.'

Mum was popular with the staff at the hospice, who always spoke of her kindness. On the days that she felt better, we took her on little adventures. I drove her around south Berkshire, to see the home that she had lived in after Chester, and we pushed her wheelchair through Valley Gardens as Barty and I hunted for chestnuts in the woods.

Eventually, the cancer made it impossible for Mum to eat, and she stopped receiving fluids into her veins. The hospice had a room for families to stay in, so Barty, Blake, Dre and I all stayed there for the last week of Mum's life, although I sometimes slept on a reclining chair in her room. Her friends came to visit, chatting to her when she was awake and sitting with her as she slept.

Barty and I went to see her first thing every morning, opening the curtains and wheeling her bed over to the window so that she could see the sun come up over the lake. It was autumn, Mum's favourite time of year, and we talked about the gradual changes in leaf colour, and watched birds migrating south for the winter.

'Don't be sad, my darling children,' she said, 'I've had a wonderful life. And I have had you two beautiful people. What more could anyone want?'

One evening I detached her bed from its plugs and moorings, and wheeled her out to the front of the hospice to see a remarkable pink and orange sunset. Jupiter and Saturn hung in the darkening sky, and Mum looked at them through the binoculars that she had given me for Christmas.

'I think this might be our last adventure together, Mum,' I said. 'I'm sorry we didn't do more.'

'Oh, we've had so many lovely times, Darling Boy,' she said. 'And this was wonderful. Thank you.'

Mum mostly slept after that, but would sometimes smile when people came in and spoke to her. She had always said that she didn't want us to be there when her final moment came because she was worried that it would be distressing for me and Barty; she would rather just quietly slip away. On her final night, I went down to her room and peeked in the window. A nurse asked if I wanted to go in, and I told her what Mum had said to me.

'It's probably not long now,' the nurse said. 'Everything is fine and normal, and it's not distressing, but you should take this chance, even if you leave the room again. Not everyone gets to do it.'

I went in and sat next to Mum, holding her hand. Her breathing had become a little harder and noisier, and her eyes were open, looking towards me.

'Hello lovely Mum,' I said, 'I hope you are doing okay. I just wanted to come in and let you know how much I love you.'

For the next little while, I shared memories of the things we had done together, and all the lovely things that she had taught me, like how to fold my socks, or the folk names of trees and flowers.

'Barty and I will always look after each other,' I said. 'We will miss you terribly, but you will always be with us. We will always love you. I know you don't want me here at the very end, so I'm just going to sit outside, and pop in from time to time. Thank you for everything, Mum. I love you.'

A single tear fell from her eye. I gently brushed it away, then kissed her on her cheek seven times, like she had done to Barty and me all our lives. I fell asleep in a chair outside her room, and a short while later the senior nurse woke me up.

'The time has come, Ash,' she said. 'Your mum has just passed away. I'll go and get your wife and sister and brother-in-law.'

We all came down and sat next to Mum's bed for a while, hugging each other. Then we did a bit of paperwork before going back to our room to sleep.

This may sound morbid, but I had been preparing for Mum's passing for a while. Her recovery from breast cancer ten years previously had made me realise how fragile life is, and how precious my mum was to me. In the years since, I had read several books about preparing for death, including *Being Mortal* by the surgeon Atul Gawande.

Gawande reflects on the illness and death of his father, and questions how we balance quality of life with length of life. He believes that modern society has become unwilling to talk about death, as if doing so will make it happen sooner. But avoiding these conversations does not prevent death; it just means that we don't talk about how we want to die.

'Endings matter,' Gawande says in the book. 'Not just for the person but, perhaps even more, for the ones left behind.'[47]

He concludes that we should put the same thought and attention into dying as we do to birth: if we have a birth plan to prepare for life's start, it seems only right that we should have a 'death plan' to prepare for its ending. While we can't determine exactly how we will die, we can let people know what matters to us before it happens.

Mum did not want to die, but she accepted that her time was limited. She intuitively understood what Gawande had written about, and gently prepared us for what was to come. At each phase of her treatment, she talked through the implications with Dre (a doctor), and then spoke to Barty and me about her wishes, all the way through to her preference for hospice care.

These conversations were unsettling, but they always ended with a sense of relief. By acknowledging Mum's mortality, rather than denying it, we were able to focus on small joys and make the most of our remaining time together. It gave us a sense of hope.

After her first bout of cancer, Mum began living her life more mindfully and enthusiastically, by seizing opportunities when they presented themselves rather than putting them off until a later date. She took that to a new level with her second diagnosis, and relished the small joys of daily life, like eating an ice cream at midnight, or having coffee with her mates. For other people, a brush with mortality can trigger more radical ambitions.

In his book *Moderate Becoming Good Later*, Toby Carr documents his sea-kayak journey through the regions of the BBC's Shipping Forecast. This is a weather programme for mariners, which divides the seas around the British Isles into 31 different areas, stretching from Iceland to the Strait of Gibraltar, and across to Scandinavia.

Toby and his twin brother, Marcus, both lived with Fanconi anaemia, a rare genetic illness that prevents the bone marrow from producing blood cells, and makes developing cancer more likely.

'At seven, I was told I would be lucky to reach 30,' Toby says in his book. 'Since reaching this milestone... I sometimes get the feeling I'm living on borrowed time.'[48]

While being treated for throat cancer in his late twenties,

Toby decided to take up kayaking and joined his local club in East London.

'[Kayaking] is easy to start and [improve] at,' he continues, 'even if you're recovering from cancer. From the moment I got in a boat, I loved the simplicity. I loved the connection I felt to the wide variety of people at the club. I loved the way it sucked me out of London and on to the wild coast around the UK. It took me away from feeling alone in the grey of the city, to being connected to nature and to others.'

As Toby's skills and knowledge grew, he went on kayaking expeditions, and then began leading expeditions himself. He went all over the UK and as far afield as Greenland, Sardinia and the Alps, taking joy in teaching others, and connecting with people from all over the world.

Then, at the age of 38, his brother passed away. Toby became acutely aware of what the future held for him.

'The numbness that engulfs me in the wake of Marcus's death subsides over summer,' he says in the book, 'and gives way to an overwhelming desire to change my life in as many ways as possible. I realise now is the time for a proper solo adventure... I don't want pity, I want to look forward because to look back is to submerge myself in the boggy ground of grief and hopelessness.'

Toby had listened to the Shipping Forecast as a child, and knew its 31 areas in that pseudomythical way of childhood memory. Now that he was a proficient sea-kayaker, the idea of visiting these places was an actual possibility. As he planned his journey around tide timetables, ferry schedules, landing spots and campgrounds, it underwent the magical transition from 'dream' to 'plan.'

'I feel butterflies,' he says in the book. 'Excited about what

242

might be possible... The end of the terrible year where I lost my brother is suddenly twinkling with the possibility of opportunity in the next.'

The expedition took Toby from Iceland to the Faroe Islands, Norway, Denmark, Germany, the Netherlands, France, Spain and Portugal. Along the way he got to know local kayakers, who helped him with advice and logistics. He learned about their lives, and the wildlife, geography, history and geology of the places that they called home. Many became his friends.

'All the late nights, storms, rough waters, difficult times and personal challenges are wrapped in the warmth of familiarity and friendliness,' he says, '[but] I always knew I was working within a window of good health.'

With just a few areas of the Shipping Forecast left to visit, Toby's illness caught up with him, and he passed away from liver cancer. His sister, Katie, decided to complete his unfinished book from his journals, and she has since learned how to kayak so that she can complete Toby's project in his memory.

Both Toby and Katie's journeys were prompted by grief, although each had a slightly different purpose. Toby wanted to live more fully, and without regret. Katie's journey is a tribute, and a way to honour and remember Toby. Both of them are suffused with a sense of hope.

Mum had a beautiful Quaker funeral in a woodland ceremonial park. Barty wrote and delivered a powerful poem and I gave the eulogy. Then the gathering sat in silence, as is the Quaker way, and anyone who had a fond memory of Mum was invited to share it with the group. A lot of people stood up and told a story of Mum's warmth and kindness. We scattered Mum's ashes in places that mattered to her and to us, such as Windsor Great Park and the River Thames. Barty took some to Australia when she moved there with Blake, and Dre and I kept some for our future garden.

In the weeks after the funeral, I felt okay. The sadness came with fond memories of Mum's fun and love. But as time went on, my grief became crippling. I was listless and uninterested in work or social events, and I felt angry at the world for continuing as normal when I knew that a catastrophe had occurred. Life would always be darker without Mum, and I wanted the world to reflect that.

Rituals around death help us to mourn, to grieve and to reinforce our social safety net. And they help us reflect on what it means to be human. But our sadness isn't resolved by a funeral, or a cremation, or a pilgrimage to a river in India. So how do you cope with ongoing grief, which the author Jamie Anderson called, 'All the love you want to give, but cannot.'?

'Grief does not end,' my counsellor told me. 'While it becomes less constant or painful with time, it often wells up again – particularly around anniversaries. You will never forget your mum, and grief reminds you of what she meant to you.'

During my pilgrimage to India with my father's ashes, I saw how travel can play a role for those who are left behind when someone dies. But, because of the difficult relationship I had with my dad, I never felt the same loss at his death as I did at the loss of my mum.

I wondered if I could discover a different type of travel after Mum's death, one which would combine aspects of both Toby and Katie Carr's journeys; a tribute, which would also help me to feel alive again.

Dr Karen Wyatt is a hospice physician and founder of the End-of-Life University, who has researched and written about grief, dying and lessons for living. She uses the term 'Grief-Travel'[49][50] and says it can take six forms:

Restorative Travel is visiting friends or family during the acute, early stages of grief; they care for you with food and shelter, until you feel ready to re-enter the world. *Contemplative Travel* is time alone, to explore your emotions, and *Physically Active Travel* helps to process emotions through exertion, such as long-distance hiking.

Commemorative Travel helps us remember a shared experience or connection with our loved one. *Informative Travel* is discovering new information by visiting a particular place, and *Intuitive Travel* is where you let yourself wander, and see what inspires or interests you. 'Intuition needs an open mind,' Wyatt says. 'But it can help you process grief through spontaneous connections and moments.'[51]

I realised that Mum had done some of these after her diagnosis – staying with friends and family, spa visits, revisiting places from her childhood, researching her family history, and letting serendipity guide her – as she dealt with the grief of losing her *own* life. Maybe that's why she was able to approach death with such acceptance.

So where could I go that would help me make sense of my own grief for Mum?

My love of travel began when I was 17 years old, when Mum sent me on that rugby tour to the Antipodes.

'New Zealand is magical,' she had said. 'I won't tell you to go, but opportunities like this don't come along very often. It's important to me that you get to have experiences like this.'

That rugby tour changed my life because it inspired the curiosity that set me on the path to travel writing, and New Zealand has remained a presence in my life ever since. Relatives moved back and forth between there and Britain, and friends like Sam Smoothy (the Kiwi skier from Chapter 6) stayed at Mum's whenever he was in England. Mum even received an invite from the official All Blacks Supporters' Club, after she chatted up their tour organiser on a train to York.

'Well, I have always thought Māori men were pretty handsome,' she said.

When Mum recovered from breast cancer, her top priority was a trip to New Zealand. She hired a camper-van with a friend, returned to the places that she had visited 40 years previously, and spent Christmas with the Smoothy family in Wānaka.

Since the beginning of our relationship, Dre had been hearing Mum and I talk about New Zealand and the impact it had on us both. So when I was offered a press trip to the country, Dre arranged to join me halfway through, so that we could explore the South Island together.

'I'm so excited for you both,' Mum had said. 'Now, when I was in Wānaka with the Smoothys, I went on the most fabulous small-plane flight over the Southern Alps to Milford Sound. It was the best thing that I have ever done, so I would like to pay for your tickets to do it.'

Things did not pan out as expected. I landed in New Zealand on 3 March 2020, and had a wonderful week in the North Island, until the tourist board sent a jetboat to find me as I was kayaking along the Whanganui River. They ordered me straight back to Auckland and stuck me on the next flight home, just before the country locked down for Covid.

After Mum passed away, Dre and I realised that there was only one place that we wanted to visit. We had already been planning to see Barty in Australia, so we started our trip with three weeks in New Zealand, with Barty joining us for a week in Wānaka.

We had someone else with us, too. Five days before the anniversary of Mum's death, Dre and I began a whole new adventure, when Dre gave birth to our daughter, Lyra. We gave her the middle name Dianne, after my mum.

At Bonz 'n' Stonz workshop in Hokitika, on the west coast of the South Island, we met Nathaniel Scott of Ngai Tahu. His iwi (tribe) had retained extraction rights for pounamu, a type of jade that has utilitarian and spiritual importance to the Māori. It only forms in the Trans-Alpine Fault of the Southern Alps, and then washes down to the west coast in the rivers.

'Europeans told us that Māori lived in the Stone Age,' Nathaniel said. 'But our stone, pounamu, holds an edge better than metal, it doesn't bend and it doesn't break. Pounamu jewellery echoes its original use as fish hooks, teething rings, and as the lethal edge on weapons. But it has esoteric properties too. It holds mana – spirit and power.'

Bonz 'n' Stonz is owned by Steve Gwaliasi, who moved to Hokitika from the Solomon Islands in the 1980s. Lyra loved him.

'It's great to have a little one in the workshop,' Steve said. 'They remind us of the beauty and joy of life. My daughter always used to bring her little one in, and she used to just sit and watch me carve. I think it helped me carve more powerful pieces.'

I asked to carve a simple piece, which I could give to Lyra when she was older.

'That's lovely,' Steve replied. 'A beautiful sentiment. Let's pick a stone. But remember that the stone picks you as much as you pick it.'

We looked at different types of pounamu, which ranges in colour from transparent green to a dark brown-and-olive mix. But Dre kept being drawn to a bright blue stone, mottled with white. It matched Lyra's eyes, which are the same colour as Mum's were. Dre has blue-grey eyes, but mine are brown, so Lyra must have inherited her eye colour on my side from her grandma.

'That's aotea,' said Steve. 'It's formed through the same geology as pounamu, but it's much rarer. I think I have a piece of it, though.'

He cut a piece of raw aotea, which I began to work on under Nathaniel's guidance, then gave a piece to Dre, which she began working on, too.

'Wow,' said Nathaniel. 'Aotea. This is the greatest treasure of my people. It can only be found on a single river, in our lands in the south. It's a great privilege to be able to safeguard it and to carve it.'

As I shaped the rough, square stone against a spinning wheel of sandstone, its dusty, rock-like appearance became a smooth translucent blue, flecked with white. The back side had a layer of green and brown that traced patterns around the blue, and I shaped it into a disc, before boring a hole through the middle. Dre had shaped hers into an oblong that got wider towards the bottom, with a tiny hole in the top.

Steve took two pieces of waxed cord and expertly hung each of the carvings on them, before tying them in knots with the skill of a sailor, and making them into two necklaces.

As we started to pack up and say goodbye, I went to pay Steve for the stone and his time.

'You can't pay me,' he said, 'it's a gift. The stone spoke to you. Or to Lyra. Besides, this felt like a special encounter. Thank you for coming here, and for sharing your story with me.'

His generosity humbled me, and we walked out in a daze with the aotea round our necks. I've not taken it off since, and Lyra always wants to play with it when I hold her.

We collected Barty from the airport and drove over the Crown Range to Wānaka. We stopped at the Cardrona Hotel on the pass, which I had visited when playing rugby for the local team. I began chatting to a farmer at the bar, and it turned out that his son had played for the same rugby club around the time that I did, so he bought us all a drink before heading back to his fields.

'This place is amazing,' Barty said. 'I can see why you and Mum loved it. It's all so cute and friendly. Like Devon, but with more spectacular scenery.'

The four of us took the flight to Milford Sound, as Mum had hoped we would, giving us views over mountains that I had explored when I lived here. One of those mountains was the ski resort of Treble Cone, where I had trained as an instructor.

When we landed back in Wānaka, we drove up the long winding dirt track to Treble Cone's control station, where crews were preparing for winter. I strapped baby Lyra to my front, and the four of us hiked to a ridge that thrust over the valley. The mighty peak of Mount Aspiring glistened with glaciers in the distance, and the chalky-blue, braided Matukituki River ran through the valley below us.

We ducked under the safety fence, and perched on a bank

of snow-grass. Barty recited the poem that she had read at Mum's funeral, and scattered some of Mum's ashes. Then I walked further up the ridge by myself.

'Hello Mum,' I said. 'You always said that Wānaka was the most beautiful place you had ever visited, and this viewpoint was my favourite place to rest when I skied here. I wish we could have come here together, but I certainly feel you here with me. Thank you for everything, Mum. All this is because of you. I love you.'

I stood up and cast Mum's ashes into the air. They caught the breeze from Mount Aspiring, and floated away in the direction of Wānaka.

Later that day I caught up with Hemi Vincent, a Māori friend who had given me a job when I lived in Wanaka. He pointed at my aotea necklace.

'Have you got a name for your taonga?' he asked. Taonga means 'treasure' in Māori, but with a deeper meaning than financial worth.

I hadn't named it, but I told him about its connection to Mum and Lyra through its colour.

'That's a strong korero,' Hemi said. 'A story. Stories have power. Can I give you a name for it?'

'I'd be honoured,' I said.

'Kia whakatomuri. Te haere whakamua,' he said. 'It's an old Māori proverb, translating as "I walk backwards into the future, with my eyes fixed on the past."'

'You see, in the Māori world, the past, the present and the future are intertwined. Time has no restrictions. The ancestors are ever-present, in both the spiritual and physical realms. Your daughter will always have her grandma watching over her, through the same eyes. And your treasure reminds you of that, always.'

Mum was right. New Zealand is a magical place. I had travelled there to help make sense of my grief, but it gave me something else. A sense of hope. Not just the simple hope that we find in all travel – the hope of something to look forward to – but a deeper feeling: that things would get better, and that Mum would always be a central part of mine and my family's life.

Through her example, Mum showed me how to prepare for the end of life. But she also showed me how to live.

In J R R Tolkien's *The Lord of the Rings*, Gandalf says, '*All we have to decide is what to do with the time that is given to us.*' Travel enriched Mum's life and mine, and I have found that it also gives me insight into myself; so I think that travel is a worthy use of the time that is given to us.

This book came about because I was travelling *less* than ever. The world was coming out of the Covid pandemic, Mum had recently passed away, and Dre was pregnant with Lyra. If I was going to travel less, then I wanted to make the most of it, so I started with a simple question: 'Why Do I Travel?'

I wrote down some of my top-line objectives for travel. Adventure. Exploration. Research. Discovery. Fun. Relaxation. To learn about the world. To learn about myself. To meet new people. To broaden my horizons.

I thought about the types of trip that I had done. Holidays. Expeditions. Training courses. Sports tours. Military operations. Business trips. Press trips. Psychedelic trips.

Then I thought about the identities that I had travelled with. Tourist. Teacher. Student. Journalist. Soldier. Grieving son.

I realised that my objectives were the *outcomes* of travel. The types of trip were the *mechanism* of travel. And the identities were something that I *became* during travel. By looking at all of them together, I began to see the underlying motivations that threaded through my journeys.

Every trip started with some form of Inspiration, and I always found Hedonistic Happiness because I love novel food. Journeys of Hardship are an exception to Hedonism, but they do provide Eudemonic Happiness, as do journeys of Service.

I began researching the motivations more deeply, with digressions into PTSD, genetic determinism, neurotransmitters and global politics. Through interviewing experts and other travellers, I saw the obvious – that our motivations evolve through experience. And, sometimes, we only notice them in hindsight.

The New Iron Curtain had a different 'flavour' of Curiosity to my previous journalistic journeys, which was rooted in my connection with the people I met. This Empathy sprang from Curiosity, but once I became aware of its attributes and features, I could apply it more consciously in future travels.

Mentorship and Healing were very specific motivations that dominated particular journeys, while Serendipity is a paradox, in that it requires me to do nothing. My research into Wonder fundamentally altered my experience of London because it stopped being something that requires distant expeditions, and instead became something that reveals everyday joy.

'Eroticism' began as 'Companionship', until I realised that travelling with a partner is different to travelling with friends. This chapter had an unexpectedly therapeutic benefit because it helped me to find new ways to love travel, within the constraints of fatherhood and marriage.

The final chapter surprised me. I thought that I had travelled to New Zealand for 'Grief'. And, yes, I remembered Mum while I was there. And, yes, I was often sad. But most of the time, I felt Mum's joyous love of life; and, for the first time in a long time, I felt that life could be good again. It was only when I researched Toby and Katie Carr's journeys that I realised the connecting thread: all three journeys took grief and transmuted it into something better. They used the alchemy of 'Hope'.

'Hedonistic Happiness' is the reason that most of us travel, most of the time. It's what we have in mind when we say 'holiday' or 'vacation'. As I've said already, there's nothing wrong with this because it fulfils many of our needs; but if we *only* travel to pursue pleasure and avoid pain, then we ignore our other motivations, and miss out on their benefits. The more conscious we become with our travel, the more rewarding it will be.

Travel has evolved enormously in the time that I have been doing it, with more people from more countries travelling more than ever before. Twenty years ago, the only sources of information were either a guidebook or word-of-mouth; now social media and websites have made everything available to everyone, all of the time.

We have to acknowledge the consequences of travel. Aviation is responsible for 5 per cent of global warming,[52] and a return flight from London to LA increases your annual carbon footprint by 25 per cent. Nor can we ignore the environmental or cultural devastation arising from some forms of tourism.

These factors require us to travel more consciously. While

we must pressure governments to enact energy transitions and environmental regulations, we have to take responsibility for our own behaviour. That means flying less, and making less damaging choices. This might make our travel less frequent and more expensive, which is another reason why we must do it more consciously. So rather than starting our travel plans by asking, 'Where do I want to go?', we should instead start by asking, 'Why do I want to travel?'

This book has suggested 12 different motivations for travel. You may find that you are drawn to some motivations more than others, and you may never encounter all of them yourself.

That's fine. They are not a bucket list to tick off, but a handrail to guide your thinking.

You might even find that this book has shown you ways to apply those motivations in everyday life. You can ask 'questions of no importance' about the town you live in. You can use 'psychogeography' when you walk to the shop. You can develop empathy with anyone. And inspiration can motivate you to learn a new skill.

Of all the experiences that travel has given me, it has most enriched my life by becoming the pathway to knowing myself and others. For all the Curiosity, Inspiration, Happiness, Mentorship, Serendipity, Hardship, Service, Empathy, Healing, Wonder, Eroticism and Hope, *that* is why I travel.

Endnotes

Introduction

1   Carl Sagan, *Pale Blue Dot: A Vision of the Human Future in Space*, New York: Ballantine Books, 1994.
2   Statista Research Department, *Weekly household spending on leisure and recreation in the UK 2020-2022*.

Chapter 1

3   Joseph Henrich and Richard McElreath. "The evolution of cultural evolution", *Evolutionary Anthropology: Issues, News, and Reviews*, 123–135.
4   Gavin Haines, "The Wanderlust Gene". *The Telegraph*, 2017.
5   LL van Lieshout, FP de Lange, and R Cools. "Why so curious? Quantifying mechanisms of information seeking", *Current Opinion in Behavioral Sciences*, 112–117.
7   I Naka et al, "DRD4 VNTR polymorphism in Oceanic populations". *The Anthropological Society of Nippon*, 2012.
8   The Waka Tapu Voyage. https://www.sciencelearn.org.nz/resources/619-the-waka-tapu-voyage
9   George Loewenstein, "The psychology of curiosity: A review and reinterpretation", *Psychological Bulletin* 75–98.

10 Will Storr, *The Science of Storytelling*, William Collins, 2019.
11 Erkan Gören, "The Biogeographic Origins of Novelty-Seeking Traits". Oldenburg Discussion Papers in Economics, No. V-366-14, University of Oldenburg.

Chapter 2

13 Isaac Newton, and Robert Hooke, "Isaac Newton Letter to Robert Hooke", 1675: https://discover.hsp.org/Record/dc-9792/Description
14 Royal Astronomical Society, "Report confirms Tim Peake's reach", *Astronomy & Geophysics*, Volume 60, Issue 1, February 2019.

Chapter 3

17 Andrew Stevenson, *The Psychology of Travel*, Routledge, 2023.
18 Paul M Fotsch, "Tourism's uneven impact: History on Cannery Row". *Annals of Tourism Research*, 2003.
19 Clarissa Elakis of ChildSafe International in *The Last Tourist*.
20 Ibid.
21 Ibid.
22 US Department of State, "Trafficking in Persons Report", 2018. https://www.state.gov/reports/2018-trafficking-in-persons-report/

Chapter 5

25 Katia Anastas, "Patrick Leigh Fermor's European Odyssey", *The Science Survey*.
26 Jan Morris, "A war hero and a travel writer of grace: Paddy was the ideal English scholar", *Observer*, 2011.

Chapter 6

27 Erin Strout, "What is 'Type II Fun" *Washington Post*, 2022.
29 Robert Macfarlane, *Mountains of the Mind*, Granta, 2003.

30   Ibid, 275–7.
31   John Geirland, "Go With the Flow", *Wired*.
32   Alan Arnette, "Everest by the Numbers: 2024 Edition". https://www.alanarnette.com/blog/2024/01/20/everest-by-the-numbers-2024-edition/
33   Mike Richard and Tom Kilpatrick, "This is how much it actually costs to climb Mount Everest". *The Manual*.
34   Zachary Crockett, "How Mount Everest became a multimillion-dollar business". *The Hustle*.

Chapter 7

36   David Nott, *War Doctor*, Picador, 2020.
37   Sebastian Junger, *Tribe: On Homecoming and Belonging*, 4th Estate, 2017.
38   *Journal of Psychosomatic Research*, Elsevier Inc, 1979.

Chapter 10

41   Dacher Keltner, *Awe: The New Science of Everyday Wonder, and How It Can Transform Your Life*, Penguin, 2023.
42   Aldous Huxley, *The Doors of Perception*, HarperCollins, 2009.
43   William Shatner, "My Trip to Space Filled Me With 'Overwhelming Sadness'", *Variety*, 2022.
44   Andrew Stevenson, *The Psychology of Travel*, Routledge, 2023.
45   Dan Kieran, *The Idle Traveller*, AA Publishing, 2013.

Chapter 11

46   Esther Perel, *Mating in Captivity*, Hodder & Stoughton, 2017.

Chapter 12

47   Atul Gawande, *Being Mortal*, Profile Books, 2015.
48   Toby Carr and Katie Carr, *Moderate Becoming Good Later*, Summersdale, 2023.
49   Etnerneva, "Grief Travel: How Vacations Can Help To Cope With

Grief". https://www.eterneva.com/resources/traveling-while-grieving

50 Karen Wyatt, "6 Types of Grief Travel – Which is Right for You?", End-of-Life University Blog, 2017. https://eoluniversityblog.com/?p=681

51 Ibid.

52 Jocelyn Timperley, "Should we give up flying for the sake of the climate?", BBC, 2020. https://www.bbc.com/future/article/20200218-climate-change-how-to-cut-your-carbon-emissions-when-flying

ACKNOWLEDGEMENTS

If I have seen further, it is by standing
on the shoulders of giants.

Why We Travel was conceived during a conversation with Levison Wood, who asked me about the most significant journeys of my life, and how they changed me. I am also indebted to Andrew J Allen, who read my first book proposal and encouraged me to push on with it.

My agent, Jo Cantello of Wolfsong Media, found Bedford Square Publishers, and I have been deeply moved by the enthusiasm and excitement that Jamie Hodder-Williams and Laura Fletcher showed for *Why We Travel*. Polly Halsey and Jacqui Lewis helped me to refine the writing, and Anastasia Boama-Aboagye, Shona Abhyankar and Jonathan Cantello helped me to get the word out. Charlotte Broster provided the author photograph, David Gati took me through the nuances of the contract, whilst Chloe Hatton, Alex Browne, Rocco

Santurri, Sophie Gwynne, Kiran Chohan, Alice Rothwell and Alex Hess helped me to refine my drafts.

I would never have done these journeys were it not for the mentors, editors and employers who gave me opportunities and advice: Peter Rawling, John Jackson, Jeff Dawkins, Louise Reznikova, Ken Lovesey, John Chapman, Matt Carratu, Julian Phelan, Nicholas Crane, Bob Mellors, Jo Payton, Jolyon Attwooll, Michael Kerr, Ben Ross, Greg Dickinson, Oliver Smith, Julian Phelan, Marcus Chidgey, Alex Rayner, Neil Bonner, Claire Clancey, Clare Davidson, Mark Polden, Pete Bull, Graham Cox and David Love.

My closest friends have supported me when I doubted my path (and not just whilst writing this book!): Andrew Allen, Pete Wright, Levison Wood, Ben Ford, Matt Sancto and David Young; and the support and encouragement of my family was vital: the extended Bhardwaj family, Lowsons, Hunts, Marshes, Thompsons and Paula Collins; Tim and Nickie Richardson, Del Butler, Ade and Cathy Okesanjo, and the Zeuschners. Katina Allen & Ina Codrington were a great support to me and my family, as were Blake Morkham-Calvert, Estelle Marsh and Sam Bhardwaj.

Thank you to the interviewees and travel-companions who made the book possible: Alberto Caceres, Emily Emmott, Jack Thatcher, Sir Chay Blyth, Gael Squibb, Libby Jackson, Ed Reeves, Bridget Mills Powell, Rob Solari, Bruce Poon Tip, Libby Brodie, Camilla and Doug Stoddart, Tom Waddington, Charlotte Barré, Davide de Jesus, Maurice Marty, Felicity Craddock, Rolf Potts, Boston Ndoole, Will Charlton, Sam Smoothy, Ben Timberlake, Lacchu Chhetri, David Wiseman, Russell Brice, Anna Chornous, Jamie Robertson, Maksym Mieshalkin, Artem Fietielia, the brave people of Ukraine, Pinki and Rajesh Saini, Leon McCarron, Isamar, Annahita Nezami, Frank White, Albin, Pachito, Steve Gwaliasi, Nathaniel Scott, Hemi Vincent, and all of the editors, public relations teams, tour operators and airlines that have supported my journalistic trips.

Many people inspired me as I developed the book, or were referenced in it: Alex Bescoby, Pip Stewart, Kate Page, my Uncle Colin, Adam Rutherford, George Loewenstein, Daisy Fan, Michael Palin, Yuval Noah Harari, Stephen Armstrong, Alain de Botton, Tim Marshall, Hannah Meltzer, Rainier Newberry, Robert MacFarlane, David Nott, Sebastian Junger, Claire Yorke, Dacher Keltner, William Shatner, Dan Kieran, Mark Mason, Alastair Humphreys, Esther Perel, Andrew Stevenson, the Thames Hospice.

But my deepest gratitude is reserved for four incredible women, who have filled my life with wisdom, joy, encouragement, and love: my sister, Charlotte 'Barty' Bhardwaj; my wife, Andrea 'Dre' Bhardwaj; my daughter, Lyra Dianne Bhardwaj; and my wonderful 'Mother B', Dianne Bhardwaj.

I am so lucky to have you in my life.

About the Author

Ash Bhardwaj is an award-winning journalist, broadcaster and keynote speaker, whose work explores the intersection of travel, current affairs and human behaviour. He has reported from around the world for outlets including the *BBC*, *Daily Telegraph*, *Sunday Times* and *Condé Nast Traveller*.

Before travel writing, Ash was a ski instructor, science teacher and wannabe cowboy. He is an officer in the British Army Reserve, and a lecturer in travel journalism at City, University of London. *Why We Travel* is his debut book.

Keep up to date with all of Ash's travels online

ashbhardwaj.com

📷 **@ashbhardwaj**

𝕏 **@AshBhardwaj**

Bedford Square Publishers

Bedford Square Publishers is an independent publisher of fiction and non-fiction, founded in 2022 in the historic streets of Bedford Square London and the sea mist shrouded green of Bedford Square Brighton.

Our goal is to discover irresistible stories and voices that illuminate our world.

We are passionate about connecting our authors to readers across the globe and our independence allows us to do this in original and nimble ways.

The team at Bedford Square Publishers has years of experience and we aim to use that knowledge and creative insight, alongside evolving technology, to reach the right readers for our books. From the ones who read a lot, to the ones who don't consider themselves readers, we aim to find those who will love our books and talk about them as much as we do.

We are hunting for vital new voices from all backgrounds – with books that take the reader to new places and transform perceptions of the world we live in.

Follow us on social media for the latest Bedford Square Publishers news.

𝕏 @bedsqpublishers
facebook.com/bedfordsq.publishers/
@bedfordsq.publishers

https://bedfordsquarepublishers.co.uk/